# THE LAWYER'S CALLING

*Christian Faith
and
Legal Practice*

**Joseph G. Allegretti, J.D., M.Div.**

*Paulist Press*

*New York • Mahwah, N.J.*

Library of Congress Cataloging-in-Publication Data

Allegretti, Joseph G., 1952–
    The lawyer's calling  :  Christian faith and legal practice  /  by Joseph G. Allegretti.
        p.  cm.
    Includes bibliographical references.
    ISBN 0-8091-3651-1 (alk. paper)
    1. Lawyers—United States.    2. Practice of law—Religious aspects. 3. Christianity and justice. I. Title.
KF298.A43  1996
241'.643—dc20                                                            96-33713
                                                                              CIP


Published by Paulist Press
997 Macarthur Boulevard
Mahwah, New Jersey 07430

Printed and bound in the
United States of America

# Contents

INTRODUCTION: The Spiritual Crisis in Law ............ 1

CHAPTER 1: Christ and the Code .................... 7

CHAPTER 2: The Profession and Vocation of Law ... 24

CHAPTER 3: Clients and Covenant ................. 37

CHAPTER 4: Prophetic Ministry ................... 51

CHAPTER 5: From Hired Gun to Healer ............ 64

CHAPTER 6: Lawyers and Litigation ............... 81

CHAPTER 7: Toward an Ethic of Care ............. 96

CHAPTER 8: A Tale of Two Lawyers ............. 110

EPILOGUE: Can a Christian Be a Lawyer? ........ 125

NOTES: ................................. 128

BIBLIOGRAPHY: ................................. 139

*For My Parents,*

*Janet and Joe,*

*With Love*

# Acknowledgments

———— ✦ ————

So many people have contributed to my thinking about the relationship between faith and lawyering that it is impossible to name them all. I must express my thanks, however, to those who encouraged me to write this book and commented upon my ideas and my writing. These include: Charles Dougherty, Anthony Fejfar, Timothy Floyd, Richard Hauser, S.J., Russell Pearce, Ruth Purtilo, Russell Reno, Jack Sammons, Thomas Shaffer, Ronald Volkmer, Wendy Wright, Jack Zuercher, S.J., and my father, Joseph Allegretti. A special thanks to Dean Larry Raful of the Creighton University School of Law for his generous support. Needless to say, I alone am responsible for defects and omissions—but I shudder at how much poorer this book would have been without the wise counsel of my friends and colleagues!

I am grateful to the students in my law school classes who read and commented upon various drafts of this book, especially Amy Faulk, who read the manuscript several times. I am indebted to my student assistants, Kristin Ostrom and Andrea Patterson, for all their hard work. This is a better book because of their long hours of able assistance. My thanks to Joan Hillhouse and Doreen Raur, too, for their expert secretarial help.

Above all, I want to thank my family for putting up with me during the months of writing, worrying, rewriting, and more worrying. My biggest supporters were my two sons, Matt and Pete, who make me proud to be a father, and my wife, Suzanne, whose gift of love brings out the best in me.

# INTRODUCTION

## *The Spiritual Crisis in Law*

———————— ✦ ————————

I told a friend that I was writing a book on the relationship between faith and the practice of law. "I'm examining what it means to be a Christian and a lawyer," I said, with a hint of pride in my voice. There was a long moment of silence, and then my friend replied, "But Joe, what will you do with the rest of the page?"

My friend's reaction is not uncommon. Frequently over the last few years, when I told non-lawyers what I was working on, I was met with a wide grin or uproarious laughter. The idea of a lawyer dealing with religious and spiritual matters—here was the lawyer joke to top them all! In contrast, my lawyer friends responded with a blank stare or a nervous chuckle. Many admitted they had not the faintest inkling what I was talking about. They could not even imagine what it might mean to explore the religious and spiritual dimensions of their work.

A few vignettes illustrate the vast gulf that separates the practice of law from the spiritual life:

> * After I had practiced and taught law for a decade, I left to attend the Yale Divinity School. I had been at the seminary only a week when another student, who had also been a lawyer, told me she had quit practicing law because "a Christian can't be a lawyer."

> * A lawyer friend of mine serves as a deacon at his church. When I praised his willingness to donate his time and talents to the church, he sighed and said, "I've got to do something on the weekend to make up for what I do the rest of the week."

> * There is a famous story, perhaps apocryphal, about a law student who, after hearing the result in a particular case, blurts out, "But that's not just!" To which the law professor responds, coldly, "If you wanted to study justice, you should have gone to divinity school!"

1

* Another law school story actually happened. A teacher asked his students what the purpose of a trial was. "To discover the truth," responded one student. The class erupted into laughter. The professor snapped, "Who cares what truth is?" "I do," said the bewildered student. "Well," said the professor, "in your discussions with God you can pursue that further." He then turned to another student and asked, "What's the purpose of a trial?"[1]

The gap between a lawyer's faith and work was not always as pronounced as it is today. The law, after all, is one of the traditional learned professions, along with medicine and ministry. The very word "profession" comes from the Latin word "to profess" or "to take a vow," and for many years the law was seen as a kind of sacred trust.

Things are different now. The legal profession is in crisis. Public esteem for lawyers has hit rock-bottom. Movies and comedians routinely garner big laughs by ridiculing lawyers. A series of highly-publicized "circus" trials, culminating in the O.J. Simpson case, have eroded public confidence not only in lawyers but in the legal system they serve. Lawyers themselves are increasingly unhappy about their career choice. As Harvard Law professor Mary Ann Glendon puts it, "American lawyers, wealthier and more powerful than their counterparts anywhere else in the world, are in the grip of a great sadness."[2]

Some statistics paint a sorry picture of the profession:[3]

* Lawyers are almost four times more likely than other people to be depressed. In a survey of 105 occupations, lawyers ranked first in depression. About one out of four lawyers experiences feelings of inadequacy, isolation, and social alienation, a far higher rate than the rest of the population.

* The pressure of billable hours has almost doubled in the last fifteen years, and now averages 2000-2500 hours a year. Forty-four percent of lawyers report not having enough time for their families; fifty-four percent don't have enough time for themselves.

* In 1990 only one-third of lawyers reported they were "very satisfied" with their work. Twenty-eight percent of male lawyers and forty-one percent of female lawyers were dissatisfied. The rates of dissatisfaction were roughly double those of 1984.

* In 1986, seventeen percent of Americans believed lawyers were less honest than others. By 1993 the figure had risen to thirty-one percent.

* In 1986, eighteen percent of people thought there were too many lawyers; in 1993 the figure had soared to seventy-three percent.

* Around half of all disciplinary complaints filed against lawyers stem from substance abuse by the lawyer. As many as thirteen to eighteen percent of lawyers abuse alcohol.

Both lawyers and non-lawyers have sought to address these problems by proposing to reform the profession. Critics often suggest taking steps to curb the increasing commercialization of legal practice and restore the traditional notion of law as a profession. Many of these proposed reforms make good sense and are long overdue.

Most discussions of the current state of the profession, however, take for granted the separation of law from the religious and spiritual side of life. Like my friends and acquaintances, critics of the profession treat it as a separate and autonomous sphere, without ties to the lawyer's deepest values and commitments. Yet by doing so they contribute to the rigid compartmentalization of life which, ironically, lies at the root of many of the problems they decry.

## A SPIRITUAL CRISIS

Let me be clear: *At its core the legal profession faces not so much a crisis of ethics, or commercialization, or public relations, but a spiritual crisis. Lawyers and the profession have lost their way.*

I speak to hundreds of lawyers and law students each year. Many are disillusioned with their work, unhappy with their lifestyle, and doubtful about the wisdom of their career choice. A sense of meaning, of service, of pride at a job well done—all these are getting harder and harder to nurture and maintain. Many lawyers tell me frankly that their role has degenerated; gone are the days when a lawyer was an independent counselor-at-law. Today, all too often, the lawyer is little more than a hired gun who feels obligated to do whatever a client wants, regardless of the lawyer's own values and morals. The very word "justice" has become the equivalent of a four-letter word, not to be used in polite conversation around lawyers.

In his examination of the current state of the legal profession, Yale Law School dean Anthony Kronman makes a similar point. Kronman says that people become lawyers for a variety of reasons. They want to make a good living, achieve personal goals, earn a respected place in the community. But they also hope that their work itself—regardless of the external benefits it may produce—will be meaningful and fulfilling. It is this belief that is in danger of disappearing today. Kronman concludes that the crisis of the profession "is, in essence, a crisis of morale. It is the product of growing doubts about the capacity of a lawyer's life to offer fulfillment to the person who takes it up. Disguised by the material well-being of lawyers, it is a spiritual crisis that strikes at the heart of their professional pride."[4]

If the crisis that besets the legal profession is primarily spiritual, then more than anything else lawyers need a way to link what they do on the job with their deepest values and commitments. They need to reconnect what they do on Monday with what they profess and pray on Sunday. There can be no cure for the malaise afflicting the legal profession unless and until individual lawyers and the profession as a whole begin to break down the walls that have separated work from faith, and approach the practice of law as an integral part of the spiritual journey. This book is intended to help lawyers do just that.[5]

I should say a few words about what this book is *not* meant to be. It is not a book about legal ethics, at least not in the narrow sense. The typical book about legal ethics analyzes in exhaustive (and exhausting!) detail the so-called codes of professional ethics that govern the profession. Such a book is basically a roadmap for lawyers to help them interpret the rules of the game and avoid getting into trouble with their state and local disciplinary agencies.

I have little interest in examining the codes of professional responsibility. In fact, I believe that ethics is more a matter of deciding *who you are* and *who you want to be* than it is a matter of learning external codes or rules. Codes serve a useful purpose, of course, which I will discuss later, but they are only a part (and a small part) of the moral life. Instead, my focus is on the larger questions of meaning that should shape our approach to work: What does it mean to be a lawyer? What does it mean to be a religious believer and a lawyer? How can I be true to my clients and the courts, while remaining faithful to myself and my God?

These are the kinds of questions that interest me and that need to be confronted if we are to reinvigorate and revitalize the legal profession. This is a book about legal ethics in that broad and encompassing sense.

This is not a book of abstract or academic theology. I write not for theologians, but for lawyers, law students, and anyone else interested in exploring the implications of Christian faith for the world of work and specifically the work of lawyers. This is a book of spirituality but not in any mystical or otherworldly sense. I think of spirituality as an *attentiveness to the presence of the sacred* in our life. One of my goals is to help lawyers cultivate an awareness of the ways in which God is present amidst their everyday activities on behalf of clients.

While I focus on the links between Christian faith and the practice of law, my perspective is not narrow or doctrinaire. I do not propose to have all the "answers" to the "problems" of being a lawyer. Nor do I believe for a moment that a simple reading of scripture or some insight gleaned from a favorite theologian will settle all the difficult issues that confront individual lawyers and the profession today. There is nothing dogmatic about my approach.

I write as a Christian because that is what I am, that is the faith tradition that I know best and that most directly nourishes my life and my spiritual journey. I am convinced that there are resources in the Christian tradition that can help lawyers reconnect their work with their deepest and most profound values. Faith can give us new ways of seeing our work and finding meaning in it.

Although I write from a Christian perspective, I believe that my reflections can prove useful to any lawyer or law student who is seeking to make connections between his or her faith and work. I have shared the ideas of this book with Christians, Jews, and Muslims, all of whom share important core religious values. Many of the themes I will explore in detail—for example, the concepts of vocation and covenant—transcend creedal or denominational differences. What is important is that each reader feel free to translate my thoughts into the language of his or her own faith-tradition. There are no experts here, only fellow pilgrims on the spiritual journey. Each of us has something to contribute, and each of us can learn from the other.

I have also discussed these issues with those who profess no religious faith. Even here, I have found more points of convergence and agreement than disagreement. Regardless of their theological differences, lawyers are *hungry* for meaning. They want their work to count for something. They want it to connect with the fundamental values that sustain them. That hunger, that desire, is all that is needed to join with me in a conversation about work and faith.

Finally, this is not a book that expends much sound and fury castigating lawyers and the profession. This is not a naysaying, doomsaying book about all that is wrong with the law and with lawyers. I have spent much of my life teaching law students and dealing with lawyers, and I know from personal experience how little is accomplished by attacking and ridiculing the decent men and women who make up the bulk of the profession. I have also met a number of lawyers who have successfully bridged the gap between their faith and their work. So this is a positive book with an optimistic message.

Lawyers *can* regain the sense of meaning and accomplishment that is too often lacking today. There *are* ways to reconnect our work with our religious values and loyalties. Our work *can* be a form of ministry to our clients and to others. As I will show, lawyers *do* have a calling to serve their God and their neighbor.

When we come right down to it, lawyers are no different than other people. They want to have a successful career, provide for their family, and contribute to their community and their world. They want to experience a sense of pride and meaning in what they do. They do not want to be one person at church on Sunday and a different, tougher, meaner person at the office on Monday. They want to be both a good lawyer and a good Christian. This book insists it is possible to be both.

# CHAPTER 1

## *Christ and the Code*

──────── ◆ ────────

What does it mean to be a Christian and a lawyer? How can we bridge the gap between our worship on Sunday and our work on Monday? At the outset it would help to have some sort of map of the terrain, some sense of the variety of options open to lawyers.

One way to orient ourselves is to examine several types or models of the Christian lawyer. We might think of these as implicit self-understandings. They are the unseen and usually unthinking ways lawyers approach their professional lives. These models shape our relations to clients, courts, and adversaries—and, most importantly, they shape how we see ourselves as lawyers. Because these models function largely at the unconscious or pre-cognitive level, they influence our thinking and our behavior without our ever realizing it.

This idea of types or models is old hat to anyone who has dipped into modern theology. It is now commonplace to point out the important role metaphor plays in religious experience. If we conceptualize God primarily as Father, for example, we will experience the divine in our lives differently than if our dominant metaphor for God is Mother, Friend, or Lover.[1] Likewise, Avery Dulles has compared and contrasted several "models of the church" and "models of revelation."[2]

Perhaps the most famous of these efforts is H. Richard Niebuhr's classic *Christ and Culture*.[3] In this pioneering work of Christian ethics, Niebuhr identified and evaluated a number of typical approaches that Christians have taken toward the wider secular culture, ranging all the way from an outright rejection of secular life in the name of Christ to a wholehearted embrace of the secular world on behalf of Christ.

As theologians know, the problem with metaphors is that they not only illuminate reality, they distort it as well. No metaphor can capture the whole of reality. Each is inadequate. God is a Father, yes, but not only a Father. The law is an ass, said Charles Dickens, but (we hope and pray) not only an ass, but also a noble instrument for the ordering of human affairs and the just resolution of disputes.

Thus it is important to examine the dominant images that shape our lives because by doing so we can lessen their hold and begin to complement them with other images that will bring to light hidden or obscure facets of reality. For example, William May has critically examined the dominant images that shape the self-understanding of physicians—images such as the doctor as parent, fighter, and technician—and argued that they should be balanced by a new image of the doctor as a teacher in covenant with his patients.[4]

In this chapter, I propose to do something similar for the legal profession. By adapting Niebuhr's typology from *Christ and Culture*, I will present several models that operate to shape the lives of Christian lawyers. Each has something to offer. Each has its weaknesses. The thrust of my argument, however, is that Christian lawyers should begin to supplement traditional images of their role with a *new* self-understanding that better integrates their faith and their work.[5]

## THE CODE

In order to critique and compare the varying self-images of Christian lawyers, we need to understand the basic norms governing the practice of law. There are two codes of professional responsibility in widespread use in America today. The American Bar Association promulgated the Model Code of Professional Responsibility in 1969 and the Model Rules of Professional Conduct in 1983. About two-thirds of the states have adopted the Model Rules, while most of the others retain the Model Code.

There are differences between the two codes, of course, but their differences fade into relative insignificance next to their similarities. Both deal with the same sorts of issues—confidentiality, conflicts of interest, litigation, advertising, etc.—and their approach to most questions is similar. For example, the two codes establish similar limits on what a lawyer can do for his client: A lawyer is not to harass an opponent, or lie, or use perjured testimony, or create false evidence.[6]

For our purposes, what is most important about the codes is the overall vision they share. Each embodies what I call the *standard vision* of the lawyer's role.

The standard vision rests on the idea that in an adversary system of justice, such as found in the United States, a lawyer's primary responsibility is to represent his client to the best of his ability and leave questions of "truth" and "justice" to others. A lawyer is the champion of his client.

This means that a lawyer should not let his own moral scruples influence his work on behalf of clients. It is none of the lawyer's business whether his client's goal is good or bad, as long as it is legal. Like the proverbial hired gun of the old west (an image I will return to in Chapter 5), the lawyer brackets his own moral values and serves as the amoral instrument of his client.

This standard vision operates both inside and outside of the courtroom. A trial is seen almost as a sporting event, where the two lawyers face off against each other, while a neutral umpire or referee (the judge and jury) enforces the rules to ensure that neither party obtains an unfair advantage.

In the same way, outside of the courtroom the lawyer functions as a neutral counselor to his clients. He is hired to give legal, not moral, advice. His job is to plan a transaction, negotiate a deal, or explain the scope and limits of the law. He should not let his own values interfere with his work but should discover what his client wants done and then do it.

We can summarize the standard vision in a phrase: The lawyer is the *neutral partisan* of his client.[7] He is neutral, in that he does not let his personal values affect his actions for clients; and he is partisan, in that he does whatever he can to achieve his client's objectives, whatever they might be, limited only by the law itself.

All lawyers are heavily influenced by this dominant paradigm. This is what the law schools teach and what the adversary system presupposes. Some lawyers rebel against it, but none can escape its force. For most lawyers, it is like the air they breathe: invisible, taken for granted, but indispensable to their daily lives.

Most importantly, this standard vision seems to provide a ready and (some believe) complete defense to criticisms of a lawyer's work:

* How can a lawyer defend the "guilty"?

* How can a lawyer help a client avoid paying taxes or evade environmental regulations?

* How can a lawyer engage in conduct that non-lawyers condemn as immoral, such as deceiving an opponent in negotiations or cross-examining a truthful witness to make him look like a liar?

In each case, the standard vision supplies a response: A lawyer serves his client as a neutral (he ignores his own values and stays away from morals) partisan (he does whatever it takes to win). Even the lawyer's choice of clients is immune from criticism. The lawyer is a neutral provider of services. Just as a physician would not refuse to treat a gangster who needs medical care, a lawyer is free to represent whomever he chooses, including the gangster.

Of course, not all persons understand or accept the standard vision. Critics argue that it *assumes* the morality of what lawyers do for clients without bothering to provide justifications. They reject the idea of the lawyer as a neutral partisan and insist that a lawyer, like other people, is a moral agent who is responsible for his actions on behalf of clients.

My purpose at this point is not to engage in a full-scale defense or critique of the standard vision. As we shall see, there are some plausible arguments in its behalf, although I maintain that no argument, no matter how weighty or sophisticated, can absolve the Christian lawyer from accountability for his actions before himself and his God.

With this background, however, we are now ready to consider a number of possible approaches that a Christian lawyer might take toward the standard vision of his role—what I will call the Code, for shorthand. Are some perspectives more compatible with Christian values than others?

## MODEL ONE: CHRIST AGAINST THE CODE

Let us consider four contrasting approaches to the Code. Remember that no one model captures all of reality. No lawyer fits snugly into just one category. Still, lawyers do have varied self-understandings, even if they are rarely articulated, and my proposed typology does illuminate the differing options open to Christian lawyers.

My first model is an adaptation of what H. Richard Niebuhr called *Christ Against Culture*. Niebuhr used the first letter of John as an example of this type. This epistle contains some of the most beautiful exhortations to love found anywhere in the bible. God is love, says the writer, and everyone who loves is begotten of God. Since God has so loved us, we must love each other. "God is love, and those who abide in love abide in God, and God abides in them" (1 Jn 4:16).[8]

At the same time, however, 1 John views the secular world as a sinful place under the domination of the powers of evil. It must be rejected for the sake of Christ. "Do not love the world or the things in the world. The love of the Father is not in those who love the world; for all that is in the world...comes not from the Father but from the world" (1 Jn 2:15-16). Each Christian is confronted with a stark choice: You are either for Jesus or for the secular world. It is black/white, either/or.

According to Niebuhr, a similar distrust of the secular realm can be found in certain strands of monasticism. Some members of groups like the Mennonites, Amish, and Shakers might fit within this category as well.

At first glance, this model might not seem to have anything to do with contemporary American lawyers. Almost by definition, those who practice law in a secular legal system can hardly be said to have renounced the world for Christ. Yet there is a way in which such thinking does influence Christian lawyers, sometimes even leading them to abandon law as a career. Applied to the legal profession, I will call this Model One, or, adapting Niebuhr's language, *Christ Against the Code*.

### Can a Christian Be a Lawyer?

I can illustrate this way of thinking with a personal story. I had been in divinity school only a week when I was sitting with a friend in the campus cafeteria. My friend introduced me to another classmate, whom I will call Linda. "You two have lots in common," said my friend. "You're both lawyers."

After exchanging pleasantries for a few moments, Linda asked me why I had left law to attend divinity school. I mumbled something about my interest in ministry and my desire to discover God's plan for me. "And what about you?" I asked.

Linda told me that she had quit practicing law because she could not square it with her religious beliefs. She had grown tired of being a hired gun whose sole loyalty was to her clients regardless of justice or morality. She told me bluntly, "I decided that I couldn't be both a Christian and a lawyer."

Here is a clear example of Model One thinking. Like Linda, persons who embrace this view insist that a Christian cannot be a lawyer. Lawyers inevitably do things for clients that no true follower of Christ could countenance. Between Christ and the Code is a chasm so wide and so deep that it can never be bridged.

This model might lead a devout Christian to reject or forsake a legal career, as did Linda. Less obviously, it can also affect the self-understanding of those who remain lawyers.

There are several ways in which Model One might exert a subtle influence on practicing lawyers. First, there is a movement among some evangelical Christians, including lawyers, to establish "Christian tribunals," divorced from the normal legal process, where Christians can bring their disputes with each other for mediation and fraternal correction. A number of Christian mediation services have sprung up around the country (a development I examine in Chapter 6).

Those who support the Christian mediation movement are not as

radical in their distrust of the law as Linda, my divinity school classmate, but they too are influenced by Model One thinking. There is
something unseemly and not-quite-right about the practice of law.
Christians should not be taking their disputes to the secular courts, and
by extension Christians should not be the lawyers bringing such cases.

Second, some lawyers admit to a vague and unsettling worry that
their work runs contrary to their faith. Each year I teach a law school
course on what it means to be a Christian (or other religious believer)
and a lawyer. I have also spoken to practicing lawyers on the subject
and participated in a number of retreats for law students. In these settings, lawyers and law students tell me of the tension they experience
between the Code and their religious values and commitments. Few if
any of them will abandon the practice of law, but the very fact that they
are wrestling with such doubts and worries suggests that they too feel
the pull of Model One.

Even if a lawyer's self-image is not affected by such thinking, the
same cannot be said of the wider culture. Law students and lawyers
are often accosted by friends or cocktail party acquaintances who find
the practice of law morally objectionable. As we all know, there is an
entire subset of cruel and biting humor that goes by the name of
"lawyer jokes." And when I was in divinity school I was asked at least
a dozen times by friends and classmates the same question that Linda
had posed, "How can you be a Christian and a lawyer?"

There is no doubt that Model One exerts an influence on lawyers
and non-lawyers alike. Now we must ask: What are the strengths and
weaknesses of this model? Must Christians take such a negative view
of the secular legal system and the work of lawyers?

### Following God in Church and Courthouse

As Niebuhr noted, one of the most attractive features about those
who hold this view is their sincerity and single-minded devotion to
Christ. These are people who put their money where their hearts are.
My classmate Linda, for example, left a well-paying and promising
career as a lawyer because of her certainty that God was calling her
elsewhere. Who would not admire such a person?

People like Linda remind us of the important role that our culture
plays in forming (and deforming) human character. Social conditions
do matter, and some environments are more conducive to living the
Christian life than others. As a parent of teenage sons, facing the daily
bombardment of MTV and peer group pressure, I can appreciate the
protest of those who denounce contemporary cultural mores as incom-
patible with their Christian values.

Yet few of us are as certain of God's demands as Linda, and few of us believe that a Christian is barred by his faith from becoming a lawyer. There are also theological objections to embracing such a narrow view. People like Linda run the risk of forgetting that sin resides not just in social structures—not just in the big bad world out there—·but in the human heart as well. There is no way to barricade yourself from evil because evil is a part of the human condition.

Furthermore, religious groups need to be in constant dialogue with the wider society both to clarify what their faith really means to them and to guard against the rigidities and excesses that insular communities are so prone to cultivate. Separate yourself from the wider community and you may have a community of saints—or you may invite the tragedies of Jonestown and Waco.

Those who renounce secular society make an even more serious error. They forget that God is at work redeeming all of creation, not only individuals or tiny communities of the righteous, and so there is no place that is beyond the reach of God's loving grace. For Christians there can be no neat division between the things of God and the things of the world, no sharp line between the realm of the sacred and the profane, because Christ came "to reconcile to himself all things, whether on earth or in heaven, by making peace through the blood of his cross" (Col 1:20).

In short, God can be found and followed not just in the church or the commune, but on our streets, in our homes, at our workplaces—even in our courthouses! As Christians we are called to be disciples of Christ in and to the world. Jesus tells us, "You are the light of the world....[L]et your light shine before others, so that they may see your good works and give glory to [God] in heaven" (Mt 5:15-16). This is the profound truth that Model One ignores.

That does not mean that Model One has nothing to say to those of us who believe, as I do, that it is possible to be *both* a good lawyer and a committed Christian. Model One plays a lesser but not insignificant role, functioning as a cautionary note for lawyers. Whenever I think of my old classmate Linda, I cannot help but wonder: Have I chosen the easier way? Have I been too quick to accommodate my religious values to the expectations of culture and the Code? Have I bought in? Have I sold out?

These are the types of questions that Model One obliges us to confront in our work. We may never resolve them satisfactorily, but we can never ignore them entirely.

## MODEL TWO: CHRIST IN HARMONY WITH THE CODE

If Niebuhr's first model rejects the secular world on behalf of Christ, his second model is the mirror image. In this way of thinking, what Niebuhr called the *Christ of Culture*, there is no perceived tension between the gospel and the world. Christian values are thought to be identical with the highest aspirations of secular culture.[9]

In this model, said Niebuhr, "Jesus often appears as a great hero of human culture history; his life and teachings are regarded as the greatest human achievement; in him, it is believed, the aspirations of men toward their values are brought to a point of culmination; he confirms what is best in the past, and guides the process of civilization to its proper goal."[10] In the life and teaching of Jesus we glimpse the goal toward which the secular world is advancing.

Perhaps the clearest exponents of this view were the liberal Protestant theologians of the nineteenth century who often seemed to picture Jesus as a Victorian gentleman who came preaching liberty, democracy, and social welfarism.

When applied to the legal profession, I call the analogous mode of thinking Model Two, or *Christ in Harmony with the Code*. Adherents of Model Two include those who envision no possible conflict between their lives as Christians and their work as lawyers. These are lawyers who consider themselves bound only by the Code.

I recall a prominent big-city lawyer I met when I was in law school. Timidly, I asked him whether he felt any misgivings when he did something for a client that violated his personal morals. He stared back at me, perplexed, and said, "It's never happened." I gave him an example we had discussed in class—you are a lawyer who knows a witness for the other side is telling the truth, but you try to make him look like a liar. Does that raise any problems? "No," he said slowly, as if talking to a simple-minded child. "That's my job. I'm hired to win."

Lawyers who adopt this model are often surprised and even a bit insulted when I ask them: Do you find it hard to be a Christian and a lawyer? Do you experience any tensions between your Christian values and your professional life? Some respond angrily: What are you suggesting? How dare you imply that being a lawyer is somehow anti-Christian! You wouldn't ask these questions of a doctor, a banker, or a plumber, would you?[11]

The reactions of such lawyers reveal their allegiance to Model Two because they refuse even to consider the possibility that the gospel might be relevant to their work and might place some kind of limits on the Code.

No one can be sure how many Christian lawyers fit into one category or another. No surveys have been taken, no polls conducted. As I was at pains to say earlier, these models are not rigid all-or-nothing categories. Many lawyers display behavior consistent with several models.

Nevertheless, on the basis of my dealings with thousands of law students and lawyers, I am certain that Model Two represents an important strand in the self-understanding of many, perhaps most, lawyers. This is hardly surprising. Although Americans love to criticize politicians, they have a deep and abiding loyalty to the democratic ideals on which this country is founded. The adversary system is part and parcel of our democratic institutions. The Constitution itself contains the guarantees of trial by jury and assistance of counsel. It is natural for American lawyers, who are taught to honor the adversary system above all else, to embrace the Code almost as an expression of divine intent.

### *The Compartmentalized Life*

What are the strengths and weaknesses of Model Two? As Niebuhr noted, this way of thinking reminds us that the world is the arena in which God's power and grace are being realized: "Jesus is the savior, not of a selected little band of saints, but of the world."[12] This model recognizes that God is at work within culture and institutions as well as individuals. The identification of the gospel message with the highest ideals of civilization has undoubtedly contributed to the efforts to create a more just and humane world.

Likewise, when applied to lawyers, Model Two has certain real benefits. By freeing lawyers from doubts about their representation, it permits them to focus with confidence on their duty to their clients. This in turn opens the door to a relationship with clients in which both parties can learn from each other and grow together. In this way, the lawyer might truly come to be a friend and companion of his client (this point is the subject of Chapters 3 and 4).

Still, there are major problems with this model. According to Niebuhr, its most serious weakness is the way it identifies the gospel with the values of secular culture. The temptation is to blunt the radical message of the gospel and domesticate its counter-cultural thrust. Jesus becomes a great moral teacher, but the scandal of the cross and the mystery of the resurrection are given short-shrift. Sin as a reality, sin that taints each of us and all of our actions and social structures, sin that cannot be overcome by any of our feeble efforts but only by the Anointed One who takes our place and dies for us—there is no place for such an unwelcome truth in the *Christ of Culture* model.

As Niebuhr so aptly put it, "loyalty to contemporary culture has so far qualified the loyalty to Christ that he has been abandoned in favor of an idol called by his name."[13] When that happens, our Christian values cease to serve as a check upon the distorted values and vain aspirations of secular society.

There are similar risks for the lawyer who lives his life in accord with Model Two. For such a lawyer, the Code constitutes the boundaries of his moral universe. As long as the Code permits him to represent a certain client or adopt a certain tactic, there are no moral questions to be raised. There is only one master at work: What the Code says he can do, he can do; what it says he must do, he must do.

In the words of the noted legal scholar Richard Wasserstrom, the lawyer comes to see himself as an "amoral technician."[14] This leads to a *compartmentalization* of life: It is as if the lawyer is one person at church on Sunday and another person at work on Monday. There is no awareness that God may call us to something *more or different* than the Code. (For example, as I will discuss in detail later, I believe that Christian lawyers are called to be not only advocates for their clients but also healers and peacemakers; they have duties not only to clients but to third-parties and even adversaries.)

The end result of Model Two thinking can be a collapse of the lawyer's moral universe, a dilution of his Christian values. To paraphrase Niebuhr, loyalty to the Code so far qualifies loyalty to Christ that he is abandoned in favor of an idol called by his name. Or, to put it more bluntly, the Code itself is invested with ultimate meaning at work, and by conferring infinite value upon a finite creation, the lawyer transforms the Code into an idol.

I suspect that if we want to understand the reason for lawyer-baiting, lawyer jokes, and the low public esteem of lawyers, we need look no further than here. Beneath the anger and the cynicism directed at lawyers lies the public's recognition that many lawyers have abdicated moral and religious responsibility for their actions. The public understands that too many lawyers see themselves as amoral technicians who act one way at work and another way at home. And the public doesn't like it.

Our assessment of Model Two must in the end echo Niebuhr's final evaluation of the *Christ of Culture* model: "It becomes more or less clear that it is not possible honestly to confess that Jesus is the Christ of culture unless one can confess much more than this."[15] Model Two does not do justice to the richness of the Christian message, the demands of the gospel, or the challenges and opportunities open to the Christian lawyer.

## MODEL THREE: CHRIST IN TENSION WITH THE CODE

I have called our first two models the mirror image of each other. This is accurate, but there is another way in which they betray a curious similarity. Neither has anything to contribute to the Christian lawyer struggling to bring his Christian values into the workplace. The first says, in effect, "Don't bother. It's not possible!" The second says, "Why bother? Just follow the Code!"

Both models adopt an either/or approach to the problem of reconciling Christ and the Code, with the first rejecting the Code unequivocally and the second accepting the Code unreservedly. But can a Christian integrate his beliefs with his work? Can he render to the Code what is the Code's, and to God what is God's? This is the central issue that our next model begins to confront.

Niebuhr talked of *Christ and Culture in Paradox*. He called the adherents of this model *dualists*, for they recognize that Christians owe their "obedience to two authorities who do not agree yet must both be obeyed."[16] Unlike those who adopt the first model, these persons reject the idea of a firm barrier between Christ and secular culture, but they do not agree with the second model either, because they deny that Christian values are tantamount to the ideals of secular society.

According to the dualist model, Christians inhabit two worlds, a private realm in which they relate to God as individuals and are bound by the teachings and example of Christ, and a public sphere where they live and work and must make accommodations to the sinfulness of the human condition. Christ and culture are in conflict, yet each must be obeyed. The Christian inhabits two worlds, subject to two inconsistent moralities.

Among Christian thinkers, we see such motifs in St. Paul, St. Augustine, and Martin Luther. Luther, for example, spoke eloquently of the Christian's duty to obey the Sermon on the Mount and return no resistance to evil, yet he also claimed that as a member of the state the Christian must sometimes be willing to take up the sword and kill. As Paul Althaus explains, Luther "establishes a sharp opposition between what the Christian does as a private person and a Christian and what he does and has to do in fulfilling the responsibility of his office in behalf of those who have been entrusted to his care."[17] This is what has come to be known as Luther's "theology of the two kingdoms."[18]

When applied to the legal profession, I call this way of thinking Model Three, or *Christ in Tension with the Code*. This group includes many of the lawyers who do not fit comfortably within Model Two and who are sensitive to the possible tension between their Christian values and their work. These are lawyers who have thought long and hard about the relation between Christ and the Code. They are even willing to concede that as lawyers they sometimes engage in conduct that a non-lawyer (and their own personal values) would condemn. In this way, they reject the underlying presuppositions of Model Two. The lawyer in Model Two knows that he can be both a good lawyer and a good Christian while the lawyer in Model Three *hopes* that it is possible to be both but *fears* that it is not.

I think of the lawyer I mentioned in the Introduction, who spends his weekends as a church deacon and who told me, "I've got to do something on the weekend to make up for what I do during the week."

The lawyer in Model Three knows no way to bring the two realms of Christ and the Code together. His only way out of the impasse is to adopt his own version of "two kingdoms" thinking. But while Luther took great pains to maintain that the realms of God and culture were not totally separate and that the Christian must affirm both in a single allegiance, the lawyer who adopts dualistic thinking is likely to compartmentalize his life. Emotionally and psychologically, it is easier to separate the two spheres of life than to hold them together in some sort of precarious equilibrium. As a result, when the lawyer is at home he tries to live out his Christian values, but when at work he looks to the Code.

Thus, despite the theological differences between Models Two and Three, the *practical effect* of adopting one or the other mindset is similar. In both cases, questions such as "How can you represent that client?" or "How can you do that for a client?" are rebuffed with the response, "I was only doing my job." In both cases, a wall is built between home and work.

The real difference between the models comes more at the emotional and psychological levels, because the lawyer who adopts Model Three must live with the unsettling realization that his work is divorced from, and sometimes antithetical to, his deepest personal and religious values.

### A Moral Schizophrenia

Niebuhr was quick to concede the virtues of the dualist model. This approach is bluntly honest about the moral ambiguities, the interwoven joys and tragedies, of everyday life. It comports with our human experience in which good and bad, grace and sin, cannot easily be separated.

Yet at the same time, Niebuhr criticized the model for its cultural conservatism. Those who live according to this model see themselves as living two lives: governed by the gospel while at home and by secular values while in the public realm of work, politics, and economics. There is little incentive to try to transform society and institutions to conform to the gospel.

We can see the same virtues and vices among lawyers who embrace Model Three. These lawyers see the moral life without illusion, as one where good and bad are often entwined and where no one can act without "dirty hands." They are willing to face the painful question whether the gospel might be in tension with or even in opposition to the Code.

Yet their approach is ultimately unsatisfying and insufficient, for it leads to a kind of moral schizophrenia. The lawyer separates his private from his public life and relegates his Christian values to the former. At work the status quo reigns.

We have all known people like this. They are good to their children. They volunteer at church. They give generously to charity. They try not to lie, cheat, or be mean-spirited. But when they get to work, they feel compelled to leave their religious values at the door. Christ is the Lord of everything except the office or the factory. There the dog-eat-dog mentality or the I'm-only-following-the-rules excuse holds sway. They forget a simple yet profound truth of the Christian message: God is the God of *all* of life, and so God's claim is on us always and everywhere. They ignore the radical edge of the gospel that judges all earthly institutions as needing reform.

Such a schizophrenic life is inherently unstable. Something has to give, and it comes as no surprise that if a lawyer takes positions at odds with his personal values, over time those values will change to comport with his public behavior.[19] Model Three slides, slowly and imperceptibly, into Model Two.

Taken to the extreme, the lawyer's role can absorb his whole personality. When that happens, he becomes like the man whose gravestone was spotted in a Scottish cemetery:

> Here lies John MacDonald
> Born a man
> Died a grocer.[20]

Born a man, born a woman—but died a grocer, a lawyer, a priest or a painter, as if work and work alone gave meaning and purpose to life.

This is the ultimate risk for lawyers whose professional lives are governed by Model Two or Three. In their inability or unwillingness to integrate their personal and professional lives, they may find the latter gobbling up the former. Some way must be found to put Christ and the Code together.

## MODEL FOUR: CHRIST TRANSFORMING THE CODE

Niebuhr's final model is *Christ the Transformer of Culture*. In some ways, this resembles his previous model, *Christ and Culture in Paradox*. It too realizes that culture is sinful, but acknowledges that Christians have obligations to the wider society.

Yet this understanding does not lead to some kind of suspended animation with the lawyer immobilized between the demands of the gospel and the obligations of society. This model is hopeful. It believes that the entire world is under the rule of Christ: Christ is at work in sinful human culture, transforming our fallen world. The gospel is seen as penetrating all of life, converting both individuals and institutions.

Niebuhr finds this motif present throughout the New Testament, especially in John's gospel, but sees it exemplified most clearly in the thinking of Augustine and Calvin. As Niebuhr says of Augustine: "Christ is the transformer of culture for Augustine in the sense that he redirects, reinvigorates, and regenerates that life of man, expressed in all human works, which in present actuality is the perverted and corrupted exercise of a fundamentally good nature...."[21]

This model also has strong biblical warrant in the teachings of Jesus about the kingdom or reign of God. Jesus teaches that the reign of God has arrived: It is present, growing like a mustard seed, rising like leaven, permeating all of life (Lk 13:18-21). It is here, in our midst, but not yet fully realized.

When applied to lawyers, I call the analogous mode of thinking Model Four, or, adapting Niebuhr's language, *Christ Transforming the Code* (for shorthand, the *Transformist Model*). Our three prior models, despite their substantial differences, have one critical point in common: they undermine the connection between a lawyer's faith-life and work-life. For Model One, there is an unbridgeable gap between Christian values and the Code. For Model Two, there is no gap at all, with the result that the lawyer's religious values provide no independent counterweight to his professional obligations. In Model Three, there is the recognition that the Christian is subject to both Christ and the Code, but this results in the compartmentalization of life, with Christ the Lord of the personal sphere and the Code dominant at work.

In sharp contrast, Model Four insists that a lawyer's faith is relevant to his work. Christ and the Code are related. Model Four asserts that Christ is the Lord of all, even the legal profession, and that Christians are called to serve Christ in all of life, even their life as professionals. It rejects the artificial separation of life into private and public spheres, with faith-commitments relevant only to the private.

Lawyer, bishop, and theologian James Pike made the point well in a lecture he gave to lawyers over thirty years ago. God has a claim on us, Pike explained, and since God is the sovereign of all of life, that claim exists at all times and in all our actions and relationships. No code, canon, or law can exempt lawyers from the sovereignty of the one true God.[22]

The task of the Christian lawyer, then, is to bring his religious values into the workplace, with the hope and trust that God will work through him to revitalize and transform his life as a lawyer, his profession, and ultimately the wider community as well.

For such a lawyer, the Code cannot be the sole guide to the moral life. The lawyer is not an amoral technician or a hired gun. He cannot avoid moral responsibility for his actions by appealing to the Code or to his professional role ("Gee, I was only doing my job"). He is a moral agent whose actions have consequences for which he is accountable, not just to himself and to others, but ultimately to God.

Rather than compartmentalize his life into neat pigeon-holes, the lawyer who embraces Model Four seeks to live an integrated life. A sign I saw on a local church makes this point succinctly: *God works through those who work.* The God I worship in hushed tones on Sunday is the God I serve in the hurly-burly of Monday.

### Breaking Down the Walls

As I examined earlier models, I was quick to point out the relative strengths and weaknesses of each. How should we assess Model Four?

It is interesting that when Niebuhr discussed his equivalent model, *Christ the Transformer of Culture*, he departed from his usual approach and failed to provide a balance sheet listing the advantages and disadvantages of the model. There is no doubt, however, that Niebuhr himself was most attracted to his final category. Most readers of his book feel a similar appeal. As one of my divinity school professors said, "Everyone wants to be a transformationist, but nobody is quite sure what it means!"

Admittedly, this is a problem with the model. Critics of Niebuhr have long commented on the slipperiness of terms like transformation and conversion. What does it really mean to say that Christ is at work *transforming* culture? What obligations for Christians follow from this? The model is notoriously vague and hard to define.

The same shortcomings apply to the *Transformist Model* of lawyering. It is the least familiar to lawyers. Its scope is unclear, its implications uncertain. Most lawyers I talk to, even those who are devout Christians, see their religious values as irrelevant to their work or as providing only vague and minimal guidance (don't lie, don't cheat). Others admit to a certain disquiet about some of the things they do, but feel they have no choice but to swallow their doubts and follow the Code. Most fit either Model Two or Three. I have known only a few lawyers who approach their work as an opportunity for transformation, an avenue of service to God and to neighbor.

My own view, however, and the foundation of this book, is that Model Four best speaks to the crisis afflicting the legal profession today. For too long lawyers have divorced their religious and personal values from their working life. Lawyers may spend twelve or more hours a day at work or involved with work—sadly, that is not uncommon—yet all the while they persist in the illusion that what happens during that time is somehow irrelevant to their spiritual life. That is a recipe for spiritual and moral suicide.

In short, the first step for lawyers—and not only lawyers, I should add—is to break down the walls that have compartmentalized their lives. They must come to appreciate and affirm that God is the God of the whole week, and that all of us are called to be disciples of Christ throughout the whole week, not just at church but at home, at work, and at play.

All our other models—despite the real strengths of each—fail at this fundamental point. They all persist in the delusion that our fundamental religious commitments have nothing to contribute to the time we spend at work. For this reason, none can serve as an adequate foundation for a Christian theology and spirituality of lawyering. At this time in history, in our present context as American lawyers, Model Four offers the most fruitful avenue for reconciling faith and work, Christ and the Code.

## INTEGRATING CHRIST AND THE CODE

What would it mean to bring the two halves of our lives together, to give Christ his due even at work, to see our professional lives not as divorced from, but as integral to, our spiritual journey? How do we begin to make real the dream of individual lawyers and a legal profession transformed by the saving power of Christ?

These are the sorts of questions I will explore in the rest of this book as I reflect upon Model Four and explore its rich implications for the practice of law. I will consider, for example, the traditional religious concepts of *calling* and *covenant*. How might they be applied to the work of the lawyer? I will examine the biblical understanding of the *prophet* and suggest several ways in which lawyers can play a prophetic role toward clients, the legal system, and society. I will analyze the role of the lawyer in litigation and will argue that the traditional Code values of partisanship and neutrality need to be balanced by a commitment to *reconciliation*. Throughout it all, I will be exploring in various ways the fundamental question of what it means to be a Christian and a lawyer.

I realize that much of what I am talking about is new and even frightening to lawyers. As I said in the Introduction, my goal is not to join the chorus of criticism aimed at lawyers today. Instead, I believe that if we begin to rethink the lawyer's role along the lines I propose, we will reduce this criticism and reclaim the proud place that the legal profession once held in the minds of many Americans. But I am less interested in the public image of lawyers than in the people—overwhelmingly good, decent people, who love their families and friends and communities, and who desire not only to do *well* at work but to do *good*—who make up the legal profession and who are groping for ways to make their work more meaningful, fulfilling, and consistent with their deepest religious convictions.

What ties together all that follows is my fundamental commitment to the ideals of the *Transformist Model*. Each of us is called to serve God in whatever we do. The goal of the Christian lawyer should be to integrate his religious values and his everyday commitments, so that his work can serve as an instrument of loving service to God and to neighbor. That is my hope and my dream. The rest of this book will suggest ways in which to transform that hope and dream into reality.

# CHAPTER 2

## *The Profession and Vocation of Law*

◆ ──────────

One way to begin to explore the implications of the *Transformist Model* is to examine the concepts of "profession" and "vocation." Despite the chorus of criticism aimed at the professions in recent years, it still appears that almost everyone is or wants to be a professional. In the classified pages of our newspapers, under the listings for "professionals," we find a bewildering variety of occupations: lawyers and dentists, of course, but also accountants and bankers, teachers and customer service agents, cosmetologists and massage therapists. Athletes are professionals, and so are drywallers.

There is a mystique about the word "professional". As Dennis Campbell puts it, "The word 'professional' is chosen to evoke an aura of respect and to elicit from those who are not professionals a confidence in the one performing the service or fulfilling the role."[1] The word conjures up images of dedication and competence. To become a professional is thought to open the door onto a world of money, status, and success.

Despite the competition today to claim the mantle of a profession, historically there were just three: law, medicine, and ministry. The word profession comes from the Latin "to profess," to take a vow or make a public declaration. Originally the word "profess" meant to take a religious vow, and a "profession" referred to the vow one took when entering a religious order. Gradually law and medicine separated from religious orders, so that by the end of the middle ages there were practicing doctors and lawyers who had not taken religious vows but who would make a solemn profession of their dedication to the ideals of their chosen field. As Stephen Barker explains, "The would-be lawyer had to profess willingness to use his mastery of the law to promote justice."[2]

### THE IDEA OF A PROFESSION

Another way to understand the concept of a profession is to identify certain traits that distinguish professionals from other workers.

Richard Wasserstrom offers a useful list of the essential characteristics of a profession:[3]

1. A profession requires a long period of formal education.
2. A profession requires more theoretical knowledge and intellectual ability than manual skill.
3. A profession is usually a self-regulating monopoly. To become a professional you must possess certain skills, but the determination whether you are competent is usually left to the profession itself.
4. A profession enjoys higher social status and better pay than most jobs.
5. A profession is involved with matters that touch the deepest concerns of human beings: matters such as material health (medicine), spiritual health (ministry), and justice (law). Professionals are not dedicated solely to their own self-interest and success; they serve a higher good. They are committed to an ideal of public service. As Roscoe Pound said in an oft-quoted definition, the term profession "refers to a group...pursuing a learned art as a common calling in the spirit of public service—no less a public service because it may incidentally be a means of livelihood."[4]
6. A profession involves an interpersonal relation between professional and client. Often the client is facing an emotionally difficult situation, is vulnerable, and has no choice but to trust the good judgment of the professional.

There is no doubt that law fits these criteria. Law requires a substantial period of formal education—high school, college, and an additional three years of law school. It is intellectually demanding. The law profession is, by and large, self-regulating. The state courts, in conjunction with the state bar associations and the American Bar Association, determine who is admitted to the profession, the standards under which they must practice, and the grounds for which they can be disciplined. Although the media periodically reports a glut of lawyers and chronicles the difficulties graduates face finding jobs, lawyers are still among the highest-paid workers in America. And while public criticism of lawyers is sharp, the social status of the profession remains high. In most families, it is still a cause for congratulations not condolences when a son or daughter becomes a lawyer! Moreover, lawyers are involved with the deepest concerns of human beings: how to live together, how to resolve social disputes peacefully, how to assure that basic human rights are preserved and protected. Finally, there is usually a human encounter between lawyer and client, in which the client, a

person or an institution with a "problem" comes to the lawyer for help
and must rely upon the character and competence of the lawyer.

In a way, of course, these basic features of a profession are norma-
tive as well as descriptive. They point to *ideals* as much as empirical
realities. Professionals are *supposed* to serve the common good and be
committed to public service, even if they sometimes fail to meet these
high expectations.

Indeed, the modern crescendo of criticism directed at the law profession can be explained in part by the public's suspicion that lawyers
have betrayed their time-honored ideals. Lawyers supposedly are only
in it for the money. They are said to be hired guns who will do anything
for their clients despite the social costs and the human suffering they
cause. On the other hand, lawyers allegedly will not hesitate to betray
their clients if it will serve their own selfish interests to do so. They are
neither honest nor trustworthy. So go the standard complaints. Public
surveys of the ethical standards of the various occupations show that
lawyers have fallen to the bottom, somewhere around members of
Congress (many of whom are lawyers) and used-car dealers.

There are many possible responses to this charge. The problem is
ignorance, some lawyers claim. The public doesn't understand what
lawyers do and why they do it (recall our discussion of the Code in
Chapter 1). Perhaps the problem is that in any lawsuit one party wins
and the other party loses, even though both are convinced *they* should
win. Or maybe the problem is a few bad apples spoiling the barrel, so
that the great majority of decent lawyers find themselves guilty by
association.

Another possibility, of course, is that the criticisms—at least some
of them, to some extent—are valid, and that there are serious problems
with the legal profession today. Some critics call for reinvigorating the
traditional notion of law as a profession, reinstilling a commitment to
serve the common good.

My approach is different. Because I am interested in exploring the
links between faith and the practice of law, I propose to shift our attention away from the idea of law as a profession and take a fresh look at
the religious doctrine of "vocation" (or "calling"; I will use the two
words interchangeably). A profession is what one professes to be, but a
vocation is what one is called to be, called to be by God. Here is a way
to begin to integrate our religious values with our work as a lawyer,
along the lines of the *Transformist Model* of lawyering I sketched in the
last chapter.

As we examine the notion of calling, we will consider three related questions. First, what constitutes a calling? Second, is the practice of law a calling? Third, if the law is or can be a calling, what are the implications for Christian lawyers?

## THE CONCEPT OF A CALLING

Christian ethicist Charles Kammer notes that in recent years the terms vocation and profession have come to signify precisely the reverse of their traditional meanings.[5] Today the word vocation is used to refer to jobs that are technical, manual, and command little status and salary. Those who don't go to college go to a vocational school to learn a trade.

Yet throughout much of western history, the term vocation signified a higher, more-exalted status. In the medieval church, for example, vocation was reserved for a specifically *religious* calling—most particularly, the monastery. Only those who renounced secular life completely to dedicate themselves to God had a calling.

Medieval theologians like St. Thomas Aquinas taught that the highest human activity was the contemplation of God. In contrast, normal secular work had no real significance, and was thought to be a hindrance to the religious life, for it distracted one from the leisure that was necessary for divine contemplation. As Lee Hardy puts it, "Those who remained outside the cloister, who remained involved in the world, may be Christian, but they were less than fully Christian."[6] People like myself, a married man with two children, were decidedly second-class Christians.

The reformation changed all this. Luther and Calvin reacted to the medieval devaluation of everyday work by attacking the notion that one could live the Christian life only by abandoning the secular world for the monastery.

Luther liberated the concept of calling from its monastic ties, abandoning any distinction between a sacred calling and profane work. No longer was a calling reserved for certain jobs. Kammer summarizes Luther's thought: "Any occupation becomes a 'calling' if its primary motive is serving God, responding to God's wishes and intentions for human existence....Luther understood that in the person of Jesus we have a model which shows that to love God is to serve the neighbor. Our vocation becomes that of loving the neighbor through our occupation."[7]

John Calvin's thinking is similar. Consider his commentary on Luke 10:38-42, the story of Mary and Martha, where one sister drops everything to listen to Jesus, and the other is distracted by her worldly chores. Calvin rejects the argument that Jesus is here favoring the contemplative over the active life. "On the contrary, we know that men were created for the express purpose of being employed in labor of various kinds, and that no sacrifice is more pleasing to God than when every man applies diligently to his own calling, and endeavors to live in such a manner as to contribute to the general advantage."[8]

Thus it is not necessary to join a monastery in order to serve God. There are no second-class Christians. On the other hand, no Christian is exempt from the duty to follow Christ and to serve the neighbor in love. There is no such thing as a calling in the abstract—no longer can we say that certain occupations are callings from God and the rest are not. Any work is a calling if—a big if—we approach it as a way of serving God and each other. Paul Althaus puts it this way: "There are no particularly holy works. Everything we do is secular. However, it all becomes holy when it is done in obedience to God's command and in the certainty that he will be pleased, that is, when it is done in faith."[9]

It's not so important *what* you do for a living—it's *how* you do it that makes the difference.

This kind of thinking goes a long way toward bringing together our worship on Sunday and our work on Monday. Neither takes precedence over the other; they are different expressions of the one single vocation to love God and each other.

### The Roman Catholic Perspective on Work

Although it was the reformers who first liberated the notion of calling from its medieval and monastic straightjacket, it would be wrong to give the impression that the Roman Catholic Church's thinking on work has remained static since the middle ages. In short, we can notice a remarkable "ecumenical convergence"[10] between Protestant and Catholic thinking on work. Although modern Catholic theology does not usually use the language of vocation, it does insist on the spiritual significance of work. Human work is seen as a participation in God's creative work.

Vatican Council II, for example, said that "when men and women provide for themselves and their families in such a way as to be of service to the community as well, they can rightly look upon their work as a prolongation of the work of the creator, a service to their fellow man, and their personal contribution to the fulfillment in history of the divine plan."[11]

Similarly, in his encyclical *Laborem Exercens*, Pope John Paul II speaks of human work as a sharing in the activity of God. According to John Paul, humans are, in a sense, co-creators with God. Furthermore, human work shares in the redemptive work of Jesus. "By enduring the toil of work in union with Christ crucified for us, man in a way collaborates with the Son of God for the redemption of humanity. He shows himself a true disciple of Christ by carrying the cross in his turn every day in the activity that he is called upon to perform."[12] Work is a way in which we participate in the cross of Jesus.

While the words are different, the sentiments are much the same. Work is important: It is an avenue by which we serve God. In Catholic terminology, work is a kind of co-creation with God; in Protestant language, a vocation.

There is much more we could say about the doctrine of vocation. There are the complexities and nuances of Luther's and Calvin's thought; the evolution of Reformed thought on vocation, especially among the Puritans; the tie between Calvinist theology and the rise of capitalism—all these and other fascinating issues to ponder. But our task is more limited: to examine the relevance of vocation to the work of lawyers. Does it make sense to talk of a lawyer's calling? And what are the implications for lawyers if they come to see their work as a calling? These are the questions to which we now turn.

## LAW AS A CALLING

Is law a calling? That is the wrong question, for, as we have seen, it is not possible in the abstract to confer the label of calling on some types of work rather than on others. Any job can be a calling because any job can be, in its own way, an instrument of Christian service. It depends upon our attitude, our disposition, not the details of what we do.

Several years ago, the noted Christian theologian James Gustafson considered whether the professions—the traditional professions of clergy, law, and medicine, as well as other emerging professions such as social work—could be considered vocations. Gustafson noted a convergence between the secular notion of a profession and the religious concept of a vocation. Professions exist to provide a service to persons and communities: "The professional institutions and those who participate in them have the end of benefiting patients, clients, and parishioners; they exist, trite as it is to say, to do good."[13] Thus while any work can be a vocation, the professions have a kind of natural propensity in that direction. Professions exist to serve others. Their very reason for being is tied up with the satisfaction of basic human needs such as health and justice.

That does not mean that every doctor or every lawyer has a vocation in the sense we have been using the term. According to Gustafson, we must scrutinize the individual practitioner's motives for entering the profession. People take up a profession like law for all sorts of reasons, and not all fit the notion of a calling. As Gustafson notes, a calling implies "some vision of better lives for individuals, for groups, and even for the commonweal of the human community." Two lawyers—or two ministers, for that matter—could do much the same work, yet for one the work could truly be a vocation, while for the other only a job.

We can explore this more fully by examining John Calvin's theology of vocation. Calvin, it might be remembered, was a lawyer before he was a theologian, and so his thinking on vocation has special interest for lawyers. Although Calvin was writing about the call to ministry, not law, there is a way in which the call of the lawyer parallels the call of the minister.

Calvin spoke of the call to ministry as having two elements.[14] First is the secret or *inner call*, the second is the *outward* call.

### The Inner Call

The inner call is the private realization that one is chosen by God to serve the church as an ordained minister. It is the witness of our own heart that we "receive the proffered office not with ambition or avarice, not with any other selfish desire, but with a sincere fear of God and desire to build up the church."

In what way might a lawyer discern a similar inner call? Over the years I have listened to hundreds of students talk about their reasons for coming to law school. Some enter law school because it is expected of them—Mom or Dad or Uncle Bill is a lawyer. Others—a good percentage—come to law school for the benefits they hope to gain. They see law school as a ticket to a healthy income and high social status.

I do not want to denigrate such practical goals. Indeed, it is notoriously difficult if not impossible to separate out the desire to do *good* from the natural human impulse to do *well*. Both play a part in many of our life choices, among them the choice of a career. Still, the desire to achieve wealth and status does not constitute a calling in Calvin's terms. To the extent that ambition and avarice are the reasons for our choice of a career, then to that extent it is simply a job we have chosen.

On the other hand, I have talked with many law students who have chosen the profession because of a dim sense that law can be a means of service to God and to neighbor. Most do not put it in these terms, of course. Sometimes students speak passionately of their moral outrage at social evils. They have come to law school to fight poverty, injustice, or pollution. Sometimes the reason is nothing more solid than a vague wish to "make things better."

I recall sitting in my office with a beginning law student and asking her why she chose to leave a good-paying job in business to enter law school. She responded timidly, almost with embarrassment: "I want to help people. I'm not sure how, but I thought law school would give me the skills to help people."

This desire to serve is at the heart of Calvin's inner call to ministry. As Gustafson puts it, our "moral motives" are part of our calling.[15] Those who enter law with the intent to bring justice to a broken world, to vindicate the rights of the weak and vulnerable, to heal broken relationships, to ensure equality to all persons—these persons have responded to a true calling. Law for them is a vehicle of service to God and to neighbor, not simply a gateway to financial and social success.

Often this wish to serve is coupled with an intuitive sense that one has the right kind of talents, attributes, and life experiences to become a lawyer. Lawyers are usually good with words; they like to speak and to write. They are often clever on their feet and enjoy a debate. They are usually precise people who value careful reasoning. I would have liked to be a major league baseball player, but even as a Little Leaguer I had a distressing inability to hit a curveball. Part of my inner call to the law was the gradual realization that the trajectory of my life—my experiences, dreams, talents, strengths and weaknesses—pointed toward the law as an arena in which I could fulfill my destiny to serve and to find meaning.

What is true for law students is equally true for practicing lawyers. Those lawyers have an inner calling who see their work not only as a good-paying job but as an integral part of the spiritual life, a place where they can use their unique talents in the service of God and the human community. As a legal aid lawyer told me, "I believe God put me here for a reason."

### The Outward Call

Calvin also spoke of the outward call to ministry. For Calvin this entailed the decision of the church to ordain a person as a minister. It is not enough to desire to serve. According to Calvin, the church should ordain only those who are of sound doctrine, live a holy life, are fit to bear the burdens of office, and have the skills necessary to discharge their heavy responsibilities.

We might think of law school as the rough equivalent of the minister's outward call. Calvin insisted that the church must assess candidates to the ministry to ensure that they have the professional skills and personal qualities required for the office. Similarly, law school is the place where students learn the skills and acquire the traits necessary for their calling. That is the reason for the classes, the clinics, and the internships.

The outward calling of the law school ensures that one has the intelligence, knowledge, abilities, and character to fulfill the responsibilities of the office. As the final step in the outward call, the law student must seek admission to the bar, take an examination, and satisfy the profession that she possesses the requisite good moral character.

Viewed from this perspective, law school is the means to an end—it is the instrument by which we develop the competencies to implement our inner call to service. It is the place where our inner call takes on flesh. Without the public calling of the law school, our private calling would remain ineffectual. Those who would serve must learn *how* to serve.

This analogy between ministry and law is not perfect. Certainly law school could do much more to help students cultivate the personal traits needed for the practice of law. As it is, legal education places so much emphasis on the acquisition of knowledge and the development of reasoning skills that it often overlooks the need for lawyers to possess a certain kind of character as well—a character that values fidelity, honesty, loyalty, and confidentiality, among other virtues.

Nevertheless, the law does bear a striking resemblance to Calvin's idea of a calling. There is both an inner call, corresponding to Gustafson's stress on a professional's "moral motives," and an outward call that confirms one's choice and provides the necessary training to exercise the calling.

I began by asking: Is law a calling? The answer is yes—but not yes in the abstract or yes in all cases. The answer is yes for those who see their work as a means to serve God and neighbor, and who pass through the testing place and training ground of law school. For those lawyers, law is not just a profession—what I *profess* to be. It is something more, a part of my religious life—what I am *called* to be by God.

## THE CALLING OF THE LAWYER

If law is or can be a calling, what are the implications for lawyers? What would it mean for lawyers to see their work as a calling?

At first glance nothing changes. The lawyer who approaches her work as a calling still spends her time meeting with clients, doing research, drafting documents, and resolving disputes. She is still regulated by the codes of professional conduct. She is still the zealous advocate of her client.

Yet in another sense *everything changes*, because the lawyer now sees herself in a different light. Her work has a different, wider frame of meaning. It has a different orientation. Her personal religious commitments and values are no longer irrelevant to her work, but are inextricably entwined with her image of herself as a lawyer and a person. As the walls between faith and work come down, the lawyer opens herself and her work to the life-changing power of God's grace. She begins to live out the Transformist Model of lawyering I sketched in the last chapter.

## A Check on Self-Interest

Charles Kammer has suggested that the concept of vocation can serve as a check upon the tendency of professionals to prefer their own self-interest to the larger good. Too often lawyers and other professionals are dominated by a small-minded concern for their own well-being. They see the profession as a means to financial and social success. Too often there is "a narrow focus upon mastering methods and procedures rather than upon the actual needs of clients or society."[16] Sometimes clients are viewed as commodities, as fee-payers rather than human beings. At the same time, lawyers can place so much emphasis on loyalty to their clients that they overlook their obligations to the legal system and to the third-parties affected by their actions.

Self-interestedness is an inevitable part of life. We are all fallible, sinful beings who cannot help but see life from our own limited perspective. But to concede the inevitability of self-interestedness is not to grow complacent about it. Some things can be done to curb or control the impulse. There is more to life than ourselves. Self-interestedness does not stop a mother from putting her life on the line to save a child in distress. It does not stop countless numbers of persons from donating their time and money to help others. It need not stop a lawyer from putting another's interests ahead of her own.

Although self-interestedness cannot be eliminated, the notion of a calling can help curb its detrimental effects. It can do so in several ways.

A sense of vocation places limits on certain behaviors that have contributed mightily to the current dissatisfaction with the profession, such as the padding of bills and the neglect of clients. A lawyer who regards herself as having a calling cannot help but see her clients differently. A client is not a mere commodity, but a human being, a human being in pain and emotional turmoil, who has come to the lawyer for help.[17] The concept of vocation opens the door to a relationship in which lawyer and client come to know each other as children of God who share a common spiritual destiny (I examine this relationship in detail in Chapters 3 and 4).

Furthermore, the idea of vocation helps put the financial and business dimensions of lawyering in proper perspective. Money and success are still important—how could they not be? But they are not the most *important* thing. Our self-worth is not bound to the size of our paycheck or our office. A lawyer has one foot in the marketplace, but if she takes her calling seriously, she also has a commitment to service that transcends the marketplace. She is governed by a higher vision. Success becomes more a matter of helping others than accumulating riches.

### Expanding the Moral Universe

There is another way in which the concept of vocation can change the way a lawyer views her work and her role. The concept of calling can broaden the lawyer's moral horizons. As the authors of *Habits of the Heart* note, "The absence of a sense of calling means an absence of a sense of moral meaning."[18] If lawyers approach their work solely as neutral partisans or hired guns, then the moral wellsprings of behavior dry up. Their moral world comes to be bounded by the desires of their clients and the technical rules of conduct governing the profession. They cease to ask *why* they do what they do.

But if a lawyer sees her work as a calling, she will necessarily confront the moral dimensions of her work. Such a lawyer is motivated by a vision of public service. She is concerned about justice and whether her actions advance or impede the pursuit of justice. She does not delude herself into believing that whatever she does for a client is somehow immune from moral scrutiny. She understands that she is a moral agent accountable for her actions, and she asks herself *why* she does what she does.

The concept of a calling gives the lawyer a kind of moral compass: it constantly reminds her that her ultimate loyalty is not to a client, or to the Code, but to God.

## A SENSE OF MEANING

The concept of calling can also help individual lawyers rediscover a sense of meaning and fulfillment in their work. As we have seen, many lawyers are facing a spiritual crisis. Many are unhappy with their work and their lives. Drug and alcohol abuse is high. A large percentage of lawyers answer with a resounding "no" when asked if they would enter the profession again if given a second chance. Many are baffled and hurt by the criticism and cruel jokes they must endure.

Others who expected to parlay their degree into wealth and status feel cheated as the glut of lawyers cuts deeply into their prospects. Too many lawyers find too little meaning in what they do.

The concept of calling has something valuable to contribute to tired, disgruntled lawyers who are wondering why they chose the law in the first place. It invites them to take a second look at what they do, to see the ways in which their work contributes to the good of individuals and society. A lawyer who assists an inventor in setting up a corporation is doing something good. A lawyer who counsels a teenager who has had his first brush with the law is doing something good. A lawyer who stands by a client undergoing a messy and protracted divorce is doing something good. A lawyer who strives to vindicate the rights of a woman unfairly terminated from her job is doing something good.

If lawyers begin to see their work as a vocation, they will find powerful resources for coping with the inevitable tensions and disappointments of their work. They will notice, perhaps for the first time, the opportunities that offer themselves to serve clients and others as a companion, helper, and healer. To the extent that lawyers locate their work in a wider, more-encompassing frame of meaning, and begin to envision it not just as a career but as a form of service linked to their Christian calling to love God and their neighbor—to that extent they will be freed from the nagging doubts about the meaning of their work. No longer will lawyers have to struggle to create a sense of meaning in what they do. Once they acknowledge the connection between their work and their spiritual life, they can embrace the meaning that was there all the time waiting to be discovered.

It is important not to be overly romantic about the notion of calling. It is no easy matter to cultivate a sense of calling when our days are a chaotic jumble of constant phone calls, impending deadlines, hurried research, endless meetings, and no-time-to-leave-your-desk-lunches. Even if we do develop a sense of calling, it will not magically cause our problems to disappear. It will not resolve all our self-doubts or nagging worries. There will still be stressful periods and painful failures.

Yet I still believe that a sense of calling can help us endure and flourish in our work. It can put things in perspective. It can give us hope. Vocation is life-giving: it reinvigorates us and helps us to link our work with those deepest spiritual values that give meaning to our lives. Ultimately, it is *transformative*.

I know this from my own career. There are times in my professional life when things go poorly—a case turns out badly, or my teaching is unsatisfactory, or I find myself so overwhelmed by the constant everyday trivia of my job that I begin to doubt whether I am in the right profession at all. When I am plagued by such doubts I cannot, by the sheer exercise of will, recapture my sense of meaning and fulfillment. But sometimes even amidst the disappointments I can see the ways in which my job does offer opportunities for service—in a quiet talk with a student after class, or a chance meeting with a colleague, or a speech to a local neighborhood group.

Sometimes I can link my work with my larger vision of myself as a person and disciple of Christ. At such times I feel the meaning returning to my work. I find myself not quite as tired or depressed, not quite as self-absorbed and fixated on my own success and accomplishments. At such times I recognize my students and colleagues not as distractions to my spiritual journey but as companions along the way, from whom I receive sustenance and to whom I in turn minister. At such times I begin to recognize, dimly, that my work is a calling, a calling from God.

# CHAPTER 3

## *Clients and Covenant*

——————◆——————

In the beginning is the lawyer-client relationship.[1]

Law is interpersonal. Lawyers represent people—or institutions like corporations, trade unions, and the like, which are made up of people and can only act through people.

A person walks into a lawyer's office. The prospective client tells a story to the lawyer. The lawyer listens and asks questions. Already there is a relationship between two people. If the lawyer takes the case, that relationship will develop. It may grow into something like friendship, or it may not. But in order for the lawyer to do a good job for his client, the relationship must be founded upon a certain mutual respect. The lawyer must gain the client's trust.

As the lawyer works for the client, their relationship may be tested. They may disagree about important matters: Should the client sign a contract? Should the client sue? Should the client testify? It is not always easy to know who is "in charge," which decisions are for the lawyer and which for the client. The parties may find themselves growing apart; there may be angry words and feelings of betrayal. The relationship may disintegrate into mutual recriminations.

The relationship between lawyer and client may go well or poorly. But there is something quite extraordinary, even mysterious, going on here, something that most of us are too blind to recognize because our eyes have grown dull and our imaginations weak: two people, each a child of God, each sinful yet redeemed, come together and for better or for worse each is moved and shaped and changed by the other.

There is a way to make sense of this relationship in religious terms. Technically, the lawyer-client relationship is a matter of *contract*— I agree to represent you for a certain fee. But the notion of contract fails to capture the reality of what is going on when lawyer meets client. Contract is how we describe a relationship between the buyer and seller of a house or a car. The relationship between lawyer and client is bigger than contract. I would call it more a matter of *covenant* than of contract.[2]

Contract is limited, external, and lives by the letter of the law; covenant is spacious, internal, and is nourished not by the letter but by the spirit of the relationship. Covenant touches the parties more deeply and intimately than does contract. It entails concern and responsibility for the other. It brings vulnerability and risk.

Not only does the concept of covenant illuminate the relationship between lawyers and clients in a way that contract does not. It has another, more important benefit: Covenant gives lawyers a way to integrate their faith-life with their everyday work on behalf of clients. It offers a bridge between worship on Sunday and work on Monday. For this reason, covenant plays an important role in the *Transformist Model* of lawyering that I espouse. Covenant is both a *description* of the lawyer-client relationship and an *ideal*. It is a reality—yet at the same time it is a goal never fully achieved but always worth striving for.

Our discussion of covenant will focus on three related issues. First, we will examine the lawyer-client relationship from the differing perspectives of the parties and indicate some of the tensions and problems that can arise when one person serves as the lawyer for another. Second, we will discuss the concept of covenant as we find it in Scripture and Christian theology. Third, and most important, we will explore the implications of covenant for the lawyer-client relationship and explain how it helps lawyers represent their clients better and integrate their Christian values more fully into their work.

## The Lawyer-Client Relationship

In any relationship the parties have a certain role to play. A parent is supposed to act one way, a child another. A doctor acts one way, a patient another. Lovers act differently than acquaintances.

The same holds true for the lawyer-client relationship. Although the roles of lawyer and client are not fixed and unchanging, there is a general core of expectations that surround each of the parties.

In general, we expect lawyers to be aggressive, tough-minded, objective, and dispassionate. They know the legal system and know how to get it to work for a client. They are expected to take charge of the relationship. Clients, on the other hand, are usually expected to be docile and passive. They are to trust their lawyer to act in their best interests. They are not to ask too many questions. They are expected to defer to their lawyer's judgment.

The analogy to the doctor-patient relationship is enlightening. If I am a patient, there is a sense in which I am in charge of the relationship: I hire my doctor and can select another if I am unhappy with the quality of care I receive. Technically, my doctor is my agent.

But the reality is quite different. Doctors make most of the important decisions. They often furnish only a cursory overview of a patient's medical condition or treatment options. Even when a doctor does take the time to explain what is happening, his language is often unintelligible to the patient. As a patient I feel anything but in charge. I show up at the office when I'm told to, undergo whatever tests the doctor orders, and usually have only the vaguest notion of why I'm doing what I'm doing.

Thankfully, this picture is changing—in large part because of legal challenges to the traditional notion of the doctor-patient relationship. But as any of us who visits a doctor knows, the traditional model is still alive and well today.

The same model governs the lawyer-client relationship, perhaps even more so, because some of the basic protections for clients, such as the doctrine of informed consent, are not as well established in the legal profession as in the medical. Few would dispute the conclusion of legal scholar Douglas Rosenthal: "The traditional idea is that both parties are best served by the professional's assuming broad control over solutions to the problems brought by the client."[3] In short, there is a way in which the lawyer-client relationship is a relationship between unequals in which the lawyer usually holds the upper hand.

### Lawyer Dominance

The reasons for this dominance by lawyers are not hard to imagine.[4] Consider just a few:

1. Clients usually come to lawyers because of some serious problem they are encountering. They are confused and troubled. This makes them vulnerable and likely to be dependent upon their lawyer.
2. Lawyers are experts. They possess certain skills and knowledge that laypersons do not. They are the guardians of the mysteries of the legal system. In contrast, clients are strangers in the strange land of the law.
3. Lawyers don't talk like other people. They use a special language, a language that clients cannot understand any more than they can comprehend a doctor's technical discussion of an illness. The use of arcane language inevitably contributes to the lawyer's dominance.
4. Because of the lawyer's expertise and the client's troubled state, the client cannot adequately evaluate how well the lawyer is doing his job. Only other professionals can determine if a lawyer is doing a

good job or a poor job. Clients have little choice but to trust their
lawyers. This explains why lawyers generally are more concerned
with how they are viewed by their colleagues than by their clients. It
also explains why *caveat emptor* (let the buyer beware) cannot be the
rule governing the purchase of legal services.
5. As we have discussed, lawyers are members of a profession and cannot help but think of themselves as members of an elite, "a special
kind of person, both different from and somewhat better than" non-
professionals.[5] The relentless challenges of law school encourage
such a mindset, and society at large contributes to the self-deception
by honoring lawyers with more financial and social rewards than
most other workers.

The result is that lawyers naturally tend to see their clients not as
whole persons, not as creatures of unconditional value made in the
image and likeness of God, but as something less, as children, perhaps,
or as broken objects that need to be fixed. Lawyer dominance often
leads to lawyer *paternalism*, the comfortable feeling that I know best
and I'm in charge.

Such a perspective discourages a full and frank dialogue between
the parties. This in turn makes it difficult to discuss moral questions
because the lawyer does not see the client as his moral equal. It
becomes easy for the lawyer to ignore his own moral values while on
the job. The lawyer comes to see himself not as a moral actor who is
responsible to his client, his conscience, and ultimately to his God—but
as a moral neuter whose work is divorced from the rest of his life and
from his deepest values. This is the problem of *compartmentalization* we
discussed earlier.

Ironically, when lawyers depersonalize their clients and see them
not as persons but as things, they also diminish the quality of their representation. A lawyer cannot do a good job when he is cut off both from
his client and from the profound wellsprings of the self.

Before leaving this rather glum sketch of the lawyer-client relationship, I should caution that not every lawyer or every client fits
these characterizations neatly. Furthermore, it is important to realize
that dominance is not a one-way street. We should not overlook the all-
too-obvious fact that lawyers depend upon their clients for their livelihood. This is true of private practitioners, who have many clients, and
it is even more true of corporate or government lawyers who are
employees receiving a paycheck. Many clients, especially businesses,
are savvy about the law system and how it works, and so they are not

as dependent upon their lawyer nor as vulnerable to manipulation. At times a client can dominate his lawyer.

When clients dominate their lawyers, however, the same kinds of problems result. Once again there is not a relationship of equality in which the two sides are open to the other. Once again moral issues are bracketed. The lawyer is encouraged to ignore the moral consequences of his actions and to do whatever the client wants as long as the client is paying.

Perhaps the problem at the heart of the lawyer-client relationship is not so much lawyer dominance (although I believe this is a major cause for worry) or client dominance (although this can and does exist). Maybe the real problem is one of the imagination: *We seem unable to envision a relationship between lawyers and clients in which one or the other is not in charge of and dominant over the other.*

As a Christian lawyer, I reject that. As a follower of Christ, I am called to see my clients as whole persons, indeed, as holy persons. I am obliged to reject both the extreme of lawyer paternalism and the polar opposite of client supremacy. I am committed to a deeper relationship with my clients in which the sacred worth of both parties is respected and honored. I am called to do more than make a contract with my client and abide by its terms. I am called to a *covenant* with my client.

## THE IDEA OF COVENANT

Covenant is an important theme in both the Old and the New Testament. Indeed, covenant is so central to scripture that theologian Joseph Allen claims it "provides a unifying theme in the midst of the multiplicity of the Bible."[6]

The Old Testament is replete with covenants between God and humans. There are God's covenants with individuals—Noah, Abraham, and David. Most importantly, there is the covenant at Sinai between God and the Israelites where the people pledge their obedience to the God who delivered them from the bondage of Egypt. Then there are the prophetic condemnations of Israel which can only be understood in light of the Sinai covenant that the people have forgotten or ignored.

In the New Testament, we witness a reinterpretation of the concept of covenant in light of the incarnation. Jesus is presented as the fulfillment of the Old Testament promises to the Israelites. Jeremiah had written of a "new covenant" written not on tablets of stone but on the hearts of men and women (Jer 31:31-34). For St. Paul, all who have faith in Christ are members of this new covenant. When believers participate in the Lord's supper, they join in the new covenant of Christ, for Jesus

himself said, "This cup is the new covenant in my blood" (1 Cor 11:25).
The promise of Jeremiah becomes a reality with the incarnation.

The God who covenants with humanity is steadfast in love. God
affirms the worth of each person, not because of anything we can do or
achieve, but because of God's love for us. God values each of us indi-
vidually, irreplaceably, and equally.[7] As God's creatures, made in God's
image, we are imbued with the capacity to covenant both with God
and with each other. *Indeed, we are called to reflect God's covenant love for
humanity in our relationships with each other.*

Thus we can talk of *human covenant* love as well as God's
covenant love. Allen suggests that human covenant love involves
seeing ourselves and other persons as belonging together in community, affirming the sacred worth of all persons without distinction,
seeking to meet the needs of others, being faithful in our commitments, and seeking reconciliation where relationships are fractured.[8]
In this way, our relationships with each other can mirror God's love
for humanity.

In light of the scriptural evidence, Allen suggests that covenant as
applied to human relationships has three core characteristics:

1. A covenant relationship arises through mutual actions of entrusting
   and accepting entrustment. Entrustment goes beyond mere trusting.
   It is "actually to place ourselves or something of value in another's
   hands."[9] There can be no covenant unless each party entrusts himself
   to the other. There is an element of risk here—when we entrust ourselves to another, we become vulnerable to betrayal.
2. A covenant is a creative act that constitutes a community in which
   the parties have responsibilities to and for each other. As members of
   the same moral community, each recognizes "that the other has
   worth, that each matters for his or her own sake, and not merely that
   each is useful. Each member of any covenant is obligated to and for
   the other members themselves, and is not merely obligated to the letter of the commitments explicitly made."[10] Covenant exceeds the letter of the law.
3. The responsibilities of covenant members continue over time. Not all
   covenants are permanent, but they do have an enduring quality
   about them. The parties undertake obligations that will not necessarily end at a specific moment in time. A parent, for example, accepts
   responsibility for a child not just today, or tomorrow, but for all the
   days to come.

We can now apply this general understanding of covenant to the unique relationship of lawyer and client. What are the obligations covenant places upon the parties? What are the possibilities it offers?

## THE LAWYER'S COVENANT

The notion of covenant is like calling in one important way: if we begin to see our work through its lens, very little seems to change, yet in a deeper sense everything is transformed.

In one sense nothing changes. Lawyers still work for clients. They are still hired to avoid or resolve problems peacefully. They still spend their time talking to clients, doing research, preparing documents, negotiating, and litigating.

Yet in another sense everything changes. The entire lawyer-client relationship rests on a new foundation. No longer does a "case" walk into my office—a tort case or a divorce case or a property case. Instead, a *person* enters my life, a person who seeks my help, a person whom I recognize as already in relation to me because I know both of us to be children of God whose common destiny is forged in our encounter with each other. My client and I belong together. Each of us is called to be faithful to the other and to serve the needs of the other.

Legal ethicist Thomas Shaffer makes the theological point well when he says that our clients are sent to us by God—"God proposes to deal with me through my client."[11] To the extent that we internalize this understanding, we are liberated from the need to see ourselves as better than our clients or in charge of the relationship. The temptation toward lawyer dominance is curbed as we come to see our clients as sent by God for our mutual conversion.

William May talks of the *reciprocity* of covenant: Each side needs the other, each side is not only benefactor but beneficiary.[12] I need my client, not only to earn a living, but also to carve out a meaningful life at work.

Let us examine again the three core characteristics of covenant love, but this time apply them specifically to the lawyer-client relationship: (1) the lawyer-client covenant arises through actions of entrustment and acceptance; (2) the parties form a common moral community in which each assumes responsibilities for the other; and (3) the covenantal relation endures over time.

## LAWYERS AND CLIENTS ENTRUST THEMSELVES TO EACH OTHER

It is easy to see how clients entrust themselves to lawyers. When a client comes to a lawyer for help, the client is usually facing some sort of serious choice or problem. Often the client is emotionally vulnerable. Most of the time the client is unfamiliar with the language and processes of the law.

The client has no choice but to place himself in the hands of the lawyer. This entrustment is inevitably accompanied by risk. The lawyer may be incompetent or negligent. The lawyer may put self-interest before client-interest. He may be more concerned with the size of his paycheck than with the quality of his representation. He may not really listen to the client's story or see the client as a human being who is confused and hurting.

Yet if we are to speak of the lawyer-client relationship as a form of covenant, then the lawyer too must make an act of entrustment, for human covenants are founded upon *mutual actions* of risk and commitment.

This is perhaps the biggest obstacle to the formation of a covenant between a lawyer and his client. Too often there is no act of entrustment by the lawyer. Sometimes this is because of the forces and factors that drive the lawyer into a position of dominance vis-à-vis his clients. It is difficult to talk of mutual risk, commitment, and trust when one party sees himself—and is seen by the other—as superior and in control.

Consider, for example, a bad experience you may have had with a physician.[13] You were confused and worried about your medical condition. As you met with the physician you could feel your level of anxiety rising. The doctor showed no interest in you as a person. He listened impatiently as you tried to explain the reason for your visit, then cut you off, asked a few questions, did a test or two, and proclaimed a diagnosis. The doctor's explanation left more questions in your mind than answers. Before you knew it, a scribbled prescription was placed in your hand and you were escorted from the office.

When the visit was over, you felt frustrated. You had taken the risk of putting yourself in another person's care, but there was no reciprocal entrusting by the physician—indeed, the physician had no interest in forging a relationship with you. To the physician, you were not so much a person in need of care as a medical "problem," a lung or a heart needing to be fixed. Under these circumstances, it would be inaccurate and downright silly to talk about any kind of covenantal relationship between you and your doctor.

Likewise, there can be no covenant between a lawyer and his client unless and until the lawyer is willing to encounter his client as an equal who has something of value to contribute to the relation. This simple willingness to meet the client as an equal is itself the fundamental act of entrustment by the lawyer. The lawyer takes the risk of entering into a human relationship with another person with all the uncertainties this entails. He may be challenged. He may be hurt. He may even be changed.

Human relationships are never easy. They often leave us disappointed, hurt, and confused. How much easier it is for a lawyer to conceive of his client not as an adult, but more like a child, or a "case" to be tried or settled. How much easier it is to take command, tell the client you'll handle everything, and then get on with your work without having to expend time and energy nurturing a relationship between equals.

It is a bit like entering a friendship.[14] This should never be done lightly. If I am your friend, I must treat you as my equal. I must be open to you. I must be willing to learn from you and be challenged by you. If I am unwilling to see our relationship in those terms, then I should not pretend to enter into a friendship that does not exist.

The indispensable first step, then, in forging a covenant between a lawyer and a client, is the willingness of both partners to entrust themselves to the other.

## LAWYERS AND CLIENTS FORM A MORAL COMMUNITY

In a covenant the partners form a common moral community in which each has responsibilities to the other. Each affirms the other as one loved by God, unconditionally, and thus possessing unconditional value. Each is answerable to the other.[15]

As we saw earlier, too often lawyers can imagine only two ways of relating to clients. Either the lawyer is in charge of the relationship, or the lawyer abdicates personal moral agency and regards himself as the unthinking instrument of the client. Ironically, these two approaches, which seem the mirror opposite of each other, betray a fundamental similarity. In both there is the assumption that one or the other party *must* dominate the relationship. Someone must be in charge, and the other party is envisioned as a robot who takes orders with no questions asked. In this way of thinking, the parties are isolated from each other. There is no chance of forging a relationship of moral equality. Neither influences the other.

This conventional wisdom has little to offer lawyers and clients in a case where the lawyer has moral doubts about a course of action. The lawyer can quit; or the lawyer can stay, suppress his moral doubts, and continue to fight as hard as he can for his client's interests.

In a covenant, however, no one is an island. Lawyers and clients are in it together. Both are moral agents seeking the best in each other. Together they are more than they are apart.

### Covenant and Conversion

In a covenant each party is open to conversion. Consider a case in which a lawyer and a client have a disagreement over a moral issue. Perhaps the client is seeking an end that is lawful but—the lawyer believes—immoral, or the client is pressuring the lawyer to adopt a tactic that the lawyer has moral objections about using. In a true relationship between equals, each is open to change, and so it is possible that the lawyer will be the agent of the client's conversion. Perhaps, after a full and frank exchange of views, the client will change his mind.

A second possibility is that the parties will explore the issue fully yet fail to reach an accord. Perhaps the lawyer will have to assert his right of "conscientious objection," as Thomas Shaffer calls it, and refuse to act further for the client. Even in such a case, insists Shaffer, something important has been accomplished, because the parties have listened to each other, been open to each other, and influenced each other in ways they might never have anticipated.[16]

But there is a third possibility as well. Perhaps *the lawyer* will change. Perhaps the lawyer's moral doubts will be dispelled as he listens to his client tell his story. Perhaps the lawyer will come to understand more fully what motivates his client, appreciate and accept the client's objectives, and choose to continue as the client's companion and lawyer.

I recall a lawyer who told me that when he began practicing law, there was one type of case he refused as a matter of conscience to accept. That was the defense of a corporation charged with violation of the environmental protection laws. This lawyer was a wildlife enthusiast, avid hiker, and camper who felt strongly about the importance of protecting the natural environment from pollution.

Several years into his law practice, however, he was approached to represent a small midwestern furniture company charged with disobeying its state environmental protection law. The company was charged with exceeding limits on the amount of sewage that could be dumped into a local river.

Somehow the company president ended up in my lawyer-friend's office. As he listened to the president talk about his dreams for his company and heard accounts of the government's heavy-handed tactics, the lawyer felt a strange thing happening: he felt himself warming to the human being who sat before him, and found himself changing his mind about representing a company in an environmental pollution action. He told the president bluntly that he would not help the company avoid its legitimate obligations under the law, but he would be willing to help it resist unreasonable regulations that might drive it out of business. The company president agreed, and said, "I'm not looking to get off if I've done something wrong, but I'm looking for someone who can help me understand what I'm supposed to do and who can make sure the state doesn't pull a fast one on me."

In that encounter my friend found himself changing. He had to abandon some of his deep-seated convictions because of the human being who sat before him and told his story. This lawyer came to know the difficult truth that the theologian Karl Barth expressed so well: "He who takes the risk of counseling must be prepared to be counseled in turn by his brother if there is need of it."[17]

If we keep in mind that lawyers and clients form a common moral community, we can understand how misleading it is to talk of their relationship solely in terms of contract. The idea of contract cannot capture the richness and open-endedness of the relationship. In fact, rather than talk of the "parties," as we do when we speak of contract, it would be more accurate to talk of the "partners" to a covenant, for the word partner signifies mutual dependence and a joint effort to achieve a common good.[18]

### The Gratuitousness of Covenant

If I see myself through the lens of contract, my focus is always on what I must do to avoid getting into trouble. Contract is minimalistic. I agree to sell you a computer, and you agree to pay a certain price. Or I agree to represent you as a lawyer for an agreed-upon fee. Each of us has specific obligations to fulfill. I owe you only what our agreement demands, nothing more. If one or the other party fails to meet its promises, we say that the contract has been breached, but there is no expectation that either party will go *beyond* the contract and serve the other in ways not demanded by their agreement.

Covenant is not so limited. Our obligations are not so easily discharged. A lawyer in a divorce action may find himself listening to his client tell stories of abuse and betrayal. What is called for is not only competent legal service, although that is always demanded, but a compassionate heart as well. The willingness to move beyond a narrow understanding of his role is the mark of the lawyer in a covenantal relationship with his clients.

As William May puts it, there is a *gratuitousness* to covenant that contract lacks: the parties go beyond the bottom-line and do things for each other because they recognize a duty to serve, not because they are affirmatively required to do so.[19] It is the difference between a seller's relationship with a buyer and your own relationship with a friend.

Consider a simple illustration. In the aftermath of the Los Angeles earthquake of 1994, some local stores were selling small bottles of soda pop for three dollars or more. If a victim of the quake was willing to spend such an exorbitant amount, there were no contractual grounds for protesting the price. This is my price, said the store—take it or leave it. *Caveat emptor*—let the buyer beware! The fact that thousands of people were without safe drinking water and had little choice but to pay the inflated price was irrelevant.

*Irrelevant in the light of contract, but not covenant.* In a covenant each party has obligations that are measured not by explicit commitments but by the *needs* of the other. Covenant places limits on the power of the more powerful to take advantage of the weaker. May argues that this is an important reason for preferring covenant to contract: "[T]he reduction of ethics to contractualism alone fails to judge the more powerful of the two parties (the professional) by transcendent standards....As opposed to a marketplace contractualist ethic, the biblical notion of covenant obliges the more powerful to accept some responsibility for the more vulnerable and powerless of the two partners."[20]

The stronger party must understand that what he does for and to the other party is judged not by the mathematical minimalism of contract but by the "transcendent standards" of God.

This talk of the professional's responsibilities to his less-powerful clients is not inconsistent with my earlier claim that lawyers should eschew lawyer dominance and treat their clients as equals. Lawyers should approach their clients as equals, but despite their best efforts, there will always be occasions when their superior knowledge and skills, and the emotional vulnerability of their clients, give them the upper-hand in the relationship. In such cases, covenant provides a check on self-interestedness and professional domination that contract does not. It reminds us that we serve our God as we serve each other.

## LAWYERS AND CLIENTS HAVE ENDURING RELATIONSHIPS

Contract usually has a fixed or limited quality to it. You sell me a car or I repair your broken air conditioner. Once I "discharge" my contract, I am released from my obligations and cease to have any duties toward you.

Covenants are more enduring. Think of a parent's relationship with her child or a husband's with his wife. There is no fixed terminal point beyond which each person's responsibilities magically disappear.

At first blush, this may seem to rule out many lawyer-client relationships. After all, while some lawyers have ongoing relationships with clients (for example, a corporate or tax lawyer providing long-term advice to a client), many others represent clients on a one-time basis (in a personal injury lawsuit, say, or a divorce). These lawyers may never see a client again once the immediate problem that brought the client to them has been resolved.

By enduring, however, we do not necessarily mean eternal (although God's covenant with humanity certainly fits that description). As Joseph Allen explains, "The responsibility may endure for a shorter or longer time, but it continues throughout the life of that covenant."[21]

So too with lawyers and clients. If I see my client as a covenant partner, I accept responsibility for the relationship, not just today or tomorrow, but for as long as it persists. This requires an unswerving allegiance to the other, a steadfastness, a constancy of devotion that continues over time. I must be faithful to this person and to our relationship.

Today the client may need a sympathetic ear; tomorrow a moral problem may arise that requires a frank and honest exchange of viewpoints, painful though this may be. Next week the client may need something else from me. But although the precise demands upon me may change, my duty of faithfulness to my partner and to our relationship endures.

Indeed, some obligations survive even the termination of the lawyer-client relationship. After the relationship ends, for example, my duty of loyalty remains, and I cannot represent a new client against a former client in the same or a similar matter. And the duty of confidentiality continues beyond the end of our relationship—even beyond the life of my former client.

By referring to the enduring quality of the lawyer-client covenant, we remind ourselves that what we do today has consequences over time. As a parent and spouse, I know that my actions have repercussions throughout the weeks and months. A word misspoken cannot easily be taken back. A small kindness may bear rich fruit later.

The same is true in the relationship between lawyer and client. The willingness to sit and listen carefully to a client's painful tale may be an instrument of unforeseen grace. It may give the client the space he needs to confront a painful choice or to move beyond a stubborn emotional impasse. A word I speak, or a gesture, or my mere presence, may take root in a client's soul and eventually blossom. Likewise, what my client says or does today may contribute to my growth in the future. Although the lawyer-client contract is finite and limited, the lawyer-client covenant has no fixed boundaries.

## THE COSTS AND BENEFITS OF COVENANT

Covenantal relationships with clients are not easy, as lawyers often remind me. Treating clients this way takes more time, some lawyers say. It leads to burnout, others warn. You feel so powerless listening to the sad stories of clients and realizing how little you can do for them; sometimes you wake up in the middle of the night and toss and turn for hours.

Yet without exception, these same lawyers insist that the benefits of such relationships far outweigh the costs. It's more personally rewarding, they explain. You feel as if you're actually connecting with someone, that what you do makes a difference. You regain that sense of vocation and service that was at the root of your decision to become a lawyer. Clients are happier about your work and more satisfied with the results when they've been treated as equal partners in the relationship. With their involvement, too, the quality of representation is higher—the lawyer has a clearer sense of the client's goals and motives, and a better picture of what the client wants and needs.[22]

If a lawyer and client see themselves as covenant partners, the lawyer is free to raise moral concerns with his client. No longer must he bracket his moral values. No longer does he have to live a compartmentalized life where his deepest values are relegated to weekends and evenings. Instead, he sees himself and his client as moral agents. Each is free to raise moral questions because each has the other's respect and trust. No longer does the lawyer have to opt for either moral dominance or moral abdication.

Covenant is an indispensable element in the *Transformist Model* of lawyering because it opens the door to a new way of relating to clients. When I come to see my client as a covenant partner, I acknowledge that here, today, in my office, in this meeting or with this phone call, while sharing a few words or a hot cup of coffee, my client and I meet on sacred ground. How could it be otherwise, when my client is a part of my spiritual destiny, and the two of us are companions on a spiritual journey?

# CHAPTER 4

## *Prophetic Ministry*

---◆---

A few years ago I presented my thinking on the lawyer's covenant to a retreat of law students and practicing lawyers. Afterward, one participant, a grizzled old corporate lawyer, approached me and said, "Covenant is a nice idea, professor, but don't forget that sometimes clients pay me to give them a good kick in the pants!"

He was reminding me in graphic terms that the lawyer's covenant with a client is not solely a matter of bringing empathy, care, and compassion to the relationship. All that is needed, of course, but there is a risk that in rejecting lawyer paternalism we may so dilute the lawyer's independent role that she becomes little more than a professional cheerleader for her client.

Sometimes what I need as a client is not just compassionate understanding but my lawyer's best judgment that what I want to do is wrong and not in accord with my deepest values. As the famous lawyer and statesman Elihu Root said, "About half the practice of a decent lawyer consists in telling would-be clients that they are damn fools and should stop."[1]

Consider again the analogy with friendship. Lawyers and clients in covenant are not precisely the same as good friends—we don't buy our friends with money!—but they are like friends in that each has the other's best interests at heart, each wants what is best for the other, and each has made a commitment to be there with and for the other. One of the things I want from a friend is a kindly ear, a compassionate smile, a willingness to listen and withhold hasty judgments.

But that is not all I want. Aren't there times when a friend—a true friend—will say to me, candidly, "Look, I think that's wrong. That's not you talking. That's not what you really want to do"? Doesn't a true friend remind me of the kind of person I want to be in my best moments, rather than blindly supporting whatever I choose in my worst moments?

This is an important element in the lawyer's *prophetic ministry* toward clients. The phrase may sound strange. Certainly it is easier to envision lawyers as priests than as prophets. Sociologists have been quick to point out that the legal system plays a cultic role as the mechanism for resolving conflicts that threaten the fabric of society. Law has its own myths and rituals, its own language, its own garb. To the layperson, the legal system can be seen as the mysterious dispenser of blind justice. In the "temple" of the law, lawyers and judges are the priests.

Yet we know from scripture—from the lives of Jeremiah, Ezekiel, and especially Jesus—that a priest can also be a prophet. The prophet is someone who interprets the signs of the times in the light of faith and speaks God's word for that time and place. The prophet calls the people back to their covenant obligations, holding up the ideal of covenant faithfulness against the reality of human faithlessness. Although prophets criticize people and institutions, they are not outsiders: they stand with the sinful, as one of the sinful, grieving as they confront the awful majesty of God's judgment.

At the same time, the true prophet holds out a vision of God's mercy and fidelity, and of the new life that is possible on the other side of judgment. As biblical scholar Walter Brueggemann puts it, prophets both *criticize* the present order of things and *energize* people with their promise of a new and transformed reality. Their task "is to bring to expression the new realities against the more visible area of the old order."[2] Prophets offer an alternative vision of the way the world could be if only people were willing to heed the word of God addressed to them in their particular time and place.

## THE LAWYER AS PROPHET

All this talk about prophetic ministry may seem to invest lawyers with an inflated sense of importance. Isn't it presumptuous and arrogant to talk of lawyers in the same breath as Isaiah, Jeremiah, and the rest of Israel's prophets?

While it is true that lawyers have not received a direct divine call to speak God's words of judgment and mercy, they resemble the ancient prophets in this way: Just as the prophets called Israel back to God and neighbor, the lawyer can be a voice calling her clients back to their better selves. The lawyer can remind clients of their deepest loves, values, and obligations.

Let me give an example. In Chapter 3 I addressed the situation where a lawyer believes that a client is seeking an immoral end or wants the lawyer to use an immoral means. I suggested that if the lawyer truly sees herself in a covenantal relation with her client, then she must be willing to accept the possibility that her own views will be transformed by the relationship. Perhaps, after talking to the client, the lawyer will find herself able to undertake a type of representation that previously she had considered off-limits.

But if this is true, so is the converse. Consider a man who comes to a lawyer with a grievance against a family member. "I want you to rewrite my will to leave my son out of it," says the client. The client is angry because of his son's announcement that he and his girlfriend are going to have a baby. Marriage is not in their plans. The client, a devout Christian with deeply traditional beliefs, responds with shock and bitterness and now sits in his lawyer's office demanding a simple change in his will.

But is it so simple? The lawyer could begin immediately to redraft the will. But if the lawyer knows the client well, and if the lawyer sees herself in covenant with her client, then her responsibilities go beyond the narrow provision of technical advice. She knows that she and the client are in a relationship where each cannot help but influence the other. Such a relationship means that each wishes the best for the other. And like any good friend, she cannot help but wonder if what her client demands, in the heat of the moment, is really in his best interests.

One possibility, of course, is for the lawyer to keep such concerns to herself, out of fear that by voicing them she will somehow interfere with her client's autonomy. Paternalism is the worry. But it does not violate client autonomy to ask, "Is that want you really want to do?" It does not interfere with client prerogatives to say, "Look, I've known you for years. I've watched you raise your kids. I know you're a good and loving father. I think you'd feel bad about yourself if you did this. Let's talk about it some more."

Ultimately, of course, the client is in charge, at least in the sense that if he wants to disinherit his son he can do so, and if his lawyer decides not to help him he can search for another who will make the change. But by speaking the prophetic word you are helping your client be the kind of person you know that he can be. You are helping your client be the kind of loving, compassionate person he is called to be by God.

Instead of merely telling a client what he can do, it is a matter of asking the client what he *should do*.[3] This is the essence of the lawyer's prophetic ministry—to encourage moral reflection. To assume the best about our clients, not the worst. To realize that we are not lonely and isolated from each other but are human beings whose lives intersect and who are called to bring the word of God to each other.

I have said that the task of the lawyer is both to *criticize* and to *energize*. I believe that it is possible to do both without paternalistically infringing upon a client, but I do not believe it is possible to do so without a prior commitment to be in covenant with the other. Again, the analogy with friendship is instructive. If I decide to do something that my friend believes is foolish, I will listen with attentiveness when my friend tells me so. But I will dismiss the criticism of an outsider, someone I do not know, as irrelevant, uncalled for, and overbearing. How dare you tell me what to do! Only if there already exists a relationship of concern and trust can I hear the words I would rather ignore.

And only if the criticism is accompanied by encouragement will there be any likelihood that I will take my friend's words to heart. The prophets of Israel accosted the people for their sinfulness, but they also held out the hope of a new reality, a new way of life that God offered to them. So too the lawyer must not only call the client to account, but give the client a new vision of how to live. This need not be done with words. Sometimes our friendship alone is enough to give our client the strength to choose wisely.

I think, for example, of the times I have had to make difficult decisions in my life. Often I have heard from my wife a prophetic word, not always spoken aloud but heard no less clearly, "Is that what you really want to do?" Always her prodding has been accompanied by encouragement in word or in deed. Just knowing that she had faith in me to make the right decision, that she would not abandon me if I chose wrongly, was enough to empower me to do what I had lacked the courage or the will to do.

### Saying No to Clients

It is also important that a lawyer learn to say "no" to clients. This is necessary not only to keep alive the lawyer's own moral values, but also because the ability to say "no" is an essential element in any true covenant. Each side must be respected; each must be given the space to be the kind of person he or she was meant to be. Neither party can be the rubber stamp of the other. Each must maintain moral accountability for her own actions but within a context of shared accountability to and for each other.

As Thomas Shaffer puts it: "There are things you will not ask your friend to do, and if your friend is your lawyer, there are things you will not ask your lawyer to do. In part—usually, I suppose—that is because you love her, and you perceive her character, and you want her to be and to become a good person. But also, I think, because you know that it would be futile to ask her. There are some things—some *lawful* things—she would refuse to do. Part of the value of her moral advice is that there are things she will refuse to do. This refusal is part of her character. Her character is what makes her your friend, and you her friend, in the first place." [4]

This too is part of the lawyer's prophetic ministry to clients. To say "I will not do this. I will not abandon you, but I will not do what you ask." And to say along with that, either openly or implicitly, "And I don't think you really want to do it either."

Finally, it is important that a lawyer raise her moral doubts with her client because these doubts do not disappear if the lawyer ignores or brackets them. Instead, the lawyer's moral misgivings go underground and fester, contaminating and subverting her dealings with her client.[5] If there is to be a true relationship of equality between lawyer and client, the lawyer must be free to voice her doubts, fears, frustrations, and resentments. To do so will not threaten the relationship; in the long run, it will strengthen it, just as Yahweh's covenant with Israel was deepened and enriched by the willingness of both sides to express honestly their disagreements and disappointments.

## PROPHETIC MINISTRY TO ORGANIZATIONS

So far we have been exploring the lawyer's prophetic ministry toward individual human clients. But lawyers spend much of their time representing organizations—everything from two-person partnerships to Fortune 500 industrial giants. Can we speak of the lawyer's prophetic ministry to such organizations?

The place to begin is with the reminder that no organization acts except through human beings. You may represent Acme Widget Company, but it is Bob Shaw or Brenda Jones whom you talk to and work with when the need arises for your good counsel. Your relationships with the human beings who act for the corporation are ripe with opportunities for forging a covenant between equals.

In some ways, it may even be easier to raise a prophetic voice when representing a corporate or organizational client than a person. Often when a lawyer represents a person in a divorce or an auto accident, the relationship between the parties does not survive the need that brought the client to the lawyer in the first place. I am in an accident. Someone sues me. I hire you as a lawyer. After the case is resolved, our relationship ends. There may be no reason for me to seek your services again.

In contrast, a lawyer often represents an organization on a continuing basis. Consider, for example, a company that hires me to give legal advice on labor relations issues. Today I get a call from the personnel office—there's a question about the job application form currently being used. Tomorrow the company may need some research on the laws protecting the disabled, or on drug testing, or on overtime scheduling. Next week I may be asked to examine the labor law implications of building a new plant or closing an old one, or opening a subsidiary in another state or country. Next month there may be a grievance arbitration under the collective bargaining contract with the union. Perhaps the company is being sued on an employment discrimination matter involving its failure to promote female workers—here I may have the opportunity both to represent the company in the lawsuit and to counsel the client on how to restructure its promotion policies to assure equal opportunity to women workers, thereby avoiding similar problems in the future.

This continuing relationship invites the parties to develop deep bonds of trust and respect, to move from contract to covenant. The lawyer comes to know the client—or, more accurately, the persons through whom the client acts—and comes to understand the complex forces that shape the company ethos and organizational culture. Over time the lawyer develops a sense of what this client stands for, what its goals are, how it treats its workers, whether it is a good or a bad place to work, how management and the board of directors interact, what kind of problems are apt to arise, how management is likely to respond, and so forth.

At the same time, the client comes to know the lawyer well. The client learns to respect and trust the lawyer. Beyond that the client comes to see the lawyer as a friend. And because the lawyer is a friend, the lawyer's words are listened to and valued, even when they are not what the client wants to hear, even when they challenge and criticize the client.

With such a history, the lawyer can often become a voice for the corporate conscience. The lawyer may be able to say, "In the past when this problem arose, you always did what you thought was right, not expedient." In such a case, the lawyer can speak prophetically because she stands alongside her client yet preserves some distance from her client.[6]

A complete outsider will not be heard. Think of what happens when a company is sued—perhaps the last person in the world who can speak a prophetic word to the company is the lawyer for the plaintiff! A true prophet criticizes *and* energizes, but an outsider's criticism will fall on deaf ears, and the outsider cannot hope to provide the company with a new vision that energizes and transforms. On the other hand, a complete insider, such as a corporate officer, is too tied up with the company to speak the prophetic word. The manager has too much invested, too much at stake. The manager may have difficulty separating her personal values and interests from the company's. A prophet can never become so comfortable that she loses the capacity for independent moral judgment. She cannot see herself as a "cog in the machine" or else she loses the independent moral perspective that is called for in times of trouble.

In contrast, the lawyer has one foot inside the company and one foot outside. She is an insider—at home with the company, trusted by the client, with a proven track record of counseling and being counseled by the client. But at the same time she remains a bit of an outsider—not as beholden to the company as its employees and able to bring a certain objectivity and independent moral vision to the issues.[7]

The lawyer can criticize and be heard. She can be a voice that says "no" when everyone else feels compelled to mumble "yes." And she can energize as well—since she knows the client well, and understands its history and traditions, she can articulate its moral ethos and can help the client see itself in new ways.

In a seminary class, one of my teachers summarized the prophetic task by saying, "Prophets comfort the afflicted and afflict the comfortable." At times a client may be sorely afflicted, and need comforting; at other times the client may be overly comfortable, and need afflicting. The lawyer in covenant with her client is uniquely poised to speak either a word of comfort or affliction, depending upon the circumstances, and depending upon the client's needs.

## PROPHETIC MINISTRY TO JUSTICE

There is a further dimension to the lawyer's prophetic ministry that needs to be addressed. Prophets have the disconcerting and upsetting habit of speaking loudly about justice and injustice. Amos, Isaiah, and the other Hebrew prophets refuse to separate worship of God from service to those too weak to help themselves. God, they insist, demands not pious rituals of religious devotion but lives lived in righteousness and dedicated to justice:

> I hate, I despise your festivals,
> and I take no delight in your solemn assemblies.
> Even though you offer me your burnt offerings and grain
> offerings,
> I will not accept them; and the offerings of well-being of
> your fatted animals I will not look upon.

> Take away from me the noise of your songs;
> I will not listen to the melody of your harps.
> But let justice roll down like waters, and righteousness like
>     an everflowing stream (Am 5:21-24).

The prophets attack all who trample the poor, turn aside the needy, exploit the vulnerable, and corrupt the legal process. What shocks the prophets is not the absence of law—Israel had quite a lot of law, thank you—but its perversion:

> Do horses run on rocks?
> Does one plow the sea with oxen?
> But you have turned justice into poison
> and the fruit of righteousness into wormwood....(Am 6:12).

It is the leaders of the people—the king, nobles, priests, false prophets, and judges—who are the special target of the prophet's anger:

> The Lord enters into judgment
> with the elders and princes of his people;
> It is you who have devoured the vineyard;
> the spoil of the poor is in your houses.
> What do you mean by crushing my people,
> by grinding the face of the poor?
> says the Lord God of hosts (Is 3:14-15).

The prophets saw what others failed to see: legal systems and structures can look fair on their face but operate unfairly and oppressively. The real problem was that those who were hurt the most were too weak to defend themselves. As the great Jewish theologian Abraham Heschel put it: "Who shall plead for the helpless? Who shall prevent the epidemic of injustice that no court of justice is capable of stopping? In a sense, the calling of the prophet may be described as that of an advocate or champion, speaking for those who are too weak to plead their own cause. Indeed, the major task of the prophets was *interference*, remonstrating about wrongs inflicted on other people, meddling in affairs which were seemingly neither their concern nor their responsibility.... The prophet is a person who is not tolerant of wrongs done to others, who resents other people's injuries."[8]

And what did the prophets expect of Israel, especially those in positions of power and privilege? In the words of Isaiah, the people are to "cease to do evil, learn to do good; seek justice, rescue the oppressed, defend the orphan, plead for the widow" (Is 1:16-17). Likewise, Jeremiah preached that to know God is to do justice to the poor and needy (Jer 22:15-16).

What would it mean to claim such a prophetic role for lawyers? How can Christian lawyers become advocates for the poor and the marginalized?

## *Legal Services for the Needy*

There are two major areas of prophetic ministry to the disadvantaged that need to be addressed. The first deals with the use of the courts to achieve justice for clients, a topic I treat in Chapters 5–7, where I examine the lawyer's role in litigation. The second, which we will consider here, involves the lawyer's obligation to provide legal services to the needy.

When lawyers accept a prophetic role, they commit themselves to the just distribution of legal services. Today in America, the poor have little access to legal counsel, and the middle-class is finding itself increasingly shut out as legal fees climb to over two hundred dollars an hour in many areas of the country. As long as we regard legal representation as a commodity like any other, no different than a TV or a toy, then those with the resources will be able to purchase legal services, and those without money will be left with no means to vindicate their legal rights.

But as the old law school saying goes, a right without a remedy is no right at all. Statutes and constitutions may guarantee a host of impressive-sounding rights, but those heavy law books are mere words on paper if people lack the means to enforce their promised rights. Under such circumstances, legal rights are nothing more than a cruel hoax, a sham perpetrated on the ignorant and the indigent.

To be fair, some measures have already been taken to ameliorate the problem. For example, indigent criminal defendants have the right to a lawyer paid for by the state. There are public defenders' offices in many cities and free legal aid clinics at many law schools. These measures are small but important steps toward assuring that the poor are not entirely bereft of legal assistance.

Furthermore, lawyers are often in the forefront of efforts to reform the legal system to make it more affordable and to guarantee legal redress to all Americans. Certainly, as part of their prophetic ministry to justice, lawyers should regard themselves as having a special responsibility to reform the legal system to make their services available to all who need them. Lawyers should scrutinize the profession carefully and ask whether certain rules (for example, the prohibitions on laypersons practicing law) exist to promote the common good or merely to serve the narrow interests of lawyers. The *Transformist Model* of lawyering summons lawyers continually to examine, critique, and work to reform our system of justice and the legal profession itself.

My concern at the moment, however, is more focused, and more limited: As an individual lawyer, in my everyday practice, how can I make a difference? As a Christian and a lawyer, what can I do?

### PRO BONO AND THE CHRISTIAN LAWYER

Many lawyers already provide uncompensated legal services to clients. Sometimes this is the result of a conscious decision to contribute a certain amount of time to what is called *pro bono publico* work—for the good of the public. Larger law firms often establish a formal mechanism to accept and distribute *pro bono* cases to their members. There may even be a lawyer in the firm whose primary job is to coordinate such efforts. Firms often proclaim proudly in their marketing literature that "last year our lawyers expended over five percent of total billable hours on uncompensated legal services," or words to that effect.

For smaller law firms or solo practitioners, efforts are less structured. I remember talking to a dentist a few years ago about *pro bono* work in his profession. He told me that a lot of his uncompensated work was simply a consequence of his patients reneging on their bills. After a certain point, he said, you have to decide whether to do everything in your means to collect the bill, even turning it over to a collection agency, or just "eat it." His own approach was not to pursue bills aggressively when he suspected that the patient had some extenuating circumstances, such as being out of work or suffering from a serious medical problem.

I have heard similar stories from lawyers. Indeed, the legal profession has institutionalized this practice, at least for some types of cases, by creating the contingency fee arrangement, whereby the lawyer gets nothing unless the client prevails, and then a fixed percentage of the recovery (traditionally, but not always, one-third).

We should not denigrate such efforts. They are well-meaning compassionate responses to a serious problem. But they suffer from the defects of all such efforts—they are sporadic, after-the-fact, gratuitous gestures that see *pro bono* as an act of charity rather than a demand of justice.

Too often in legal circles the question of *pro bono* is dealt with as just another proposed regulation, and so the discussion focuses on technical, "legalistic" questions: Should *pro bono* be mandatory or permissive? Is it akin to slavery, as many lawyers hyperbolically object, or is it a natural correlate of belonging to a learned profession that is afforded substantial autonomy and status by society? If *pro bono* is made mandatory, how will the duty be enforced? How many hours will a lawyer have to donate each year? Could a lawyer buy her way out of the requirement by making a cash donation to a local legal aid clinic? If so, at what rate? The questions multiply as lawyers turn their fertile, disputatious minds to the problem. Soon the underlying issue of the lawyer's duty to serve gets lost amidst the hair-splitting and the angels-on-the-head-of-a-pin counting.

For the Christian lawyer, the issue of *pro bono* should be approached from a different perspective. The question is not: Can the legal profession *make me* donate my time and talent without recompense? The question is rather: How can I best fulfill my calling to serve my neighbor in distress? As we have seen, the notion of a calling includes a duty to see beyond the self, to move from self-interestedness to selflessness, to commit ourselves to making the world a better place to live for people and for communities.

The prophetic dimension of lawyering adds a further wrinkle, for it obligates the lawyer to take special account of those who lack the power and the resources to stand up for themselves. For the Christian lawyer, *pro bono* can never be simply a matter of charity. It is not something *extra* that I do in addition to my other more-important and lucrative work. It is not the icing on the cake. It is what God expects of me. No, the point must be made more strongly—it is what God *demands* of me. To repeat Jeremiah's challenge: If we are to know God, we must do justice to the poor and needy. As Heschel puts it, "to do justice is what God demands of every [person]: it is the supreme commandment, and one that cannot be fulfilled vicariously."[9]

If we fail to serve the poor, we place ourselves in the company of the priests and the leaders whom the prophets castigated. We are guilty of perverting the legal system, of promising justice but not delivering, of turning a deaf ear and a blind eye to the wrongs suffered by those who lack the resources to protect themselves. The prophet, says Heschel, is the advocate for those who cannot speak for themselves. The question Heschel asks—Who will plead for the helpless?—can only be answered one way: each of us, in our own way, in our own place. For the lawyer, that entails some sort of legal work on behalf of the needy.

As a lawyer I can begin to cultivate this perspective by engaging in an intentional act of prayerful soul-searching (an act of *discernment*, as my Jesuit colleagues are wont to say). I know that I am called in my professional life to minister to the needy. How can I do this? Where are my opportunities? What fits my temperament and talents?

Just as not all of us are called to hands-on work with the poor in a local soup kitchen, not all lawyers are called to provide free criminal defense work or free immigration counseling for the poor. A calling, as we have seen, reflects the trajectory of *my* life, *my* skills and abilities, *my* values and dreams.

Some lawyers may provide free legal advice to clients. Some may work on a bar committee to increase access to the legal system. Other lawyers may be trained as mediators to resolve family disputes or other quarrels without the need to go to court. Some may serve on the boards of directors of local groups that serve the poor. Others may donate their time and energy to reforming the civil rights laws or land-lord-tenant laws to assure equal rights for all persons in the community. The opportunities are as varied as the individuals who make up the legal profession.

It is not as important what I do as that I do *something*. Justice, after all, is a big country, and many are the roads that lead there. I may do little, at least at first, but that is not the point either. What is important is that I engage in prayerful reflection and then make an intentional decision to open myself to the needy. By making such a decision, my works of justice on behalf of the disadvantaged and marginalized become integrated into my overall vision of my work. They become part of who I am as a lawyer and a person.

I recall a lawyer I knew years ago. She worked in a major Wall-Street-type law firm doing corporate taxation. One day the firm received a request for a lawyer to sit on a local committee that was examining state laws on the status of the mentally retarded. She volunteered to attend one meeting of the committee. At the meeting she was shocked to learn that her state law provided almost no legal protections for the retarded. Many people were institutionalized without formal judicial proceedings. Basic due process protections were nonexistent. The lawyer's moral outrage at the wrongs being perpetrated on the powerless led her to help draft new legislation affording basic legal protections to the retarded. She spent several years and countless hours lobbying until her proposed legislation was finally enacted into law. Years later I heard from a mutual friend that she now sat on the board of directors of a national disability rights advocacy group.

All because of a willingness to go to a single meeting.

This is a dramatic example, of course, but it illustrates a more mundane point. As I begin to open my heart to my neighbors in need—

as I hear their stories and come to know them not as numbing statistics but as people no different than myself—I begin a journey that is not under my direct control but is part of God's loving plan for me. It may lead me in strange and frightening directions. It may upset my entire life. I may never be the same. But along the way I may find myself.

# CHAPTER 5

## *From Hired Gun to Healer*

———————◆———————

A friend of mine tells a story about his first case as an associate in a large midwestern law firm. The case involved a complex business deal that broke down, leading to mutual recriminations and eventually to each of the parties suing the other. My friend was assigned to work with two more-senior lawyers. At the first meeting of the team, the partner in charge said, "We have no interest in winning this case in court. Our job is to make life so miserable for the other side that they'll settle. I want every possible motion filed, I want you to object to every request for information, I want you to make our opponent's life a living hell."

A second incident dates from the time when I was leaving legal practice to become a teacher. A lawyer from another firm whom I knew only slightly called and invited me to lunch. At lunch he told me that he too was interested in teaching. I asked him why he wanted to leave his successful litigation practice and go into teaching. He gave me all the usual reasons—he wanted more time to think about legal issues, he hoped for the opportunity to reform the law, he had always wanted to teach. But when he was done, he looked at me and said, "But the real reason is that I don't like the kind of person I've become."

"What do you mean?" I asked. I knew him to be a tough combative litigator who was well-respected by clients and lawyers.

"I spend all my time treating people like dirt," he said, "and then when I go home I'm tough on my wife and kids, like I'm itching for a fight. It's hard to be an SOB all day and leave it at the office."

Finally, there is the story of Sam Benson, a Colorado lawyer, who quit practicing law and wrote in Newsweek: "I was tired of the deceit. I was tired of the chicanery. But most of all, I was tired of the misery my job caused other people."[1] Benson is not alone. An estimated 40,000 lawyers drop out of practice each year.[2]

These vignettes could be multiplied infinitely. Each raises in its own way the moral costs and problems associated with representing a client in litigation. Conflicts and tensions between a lawyer's personal values and his duties to his clients may arise in any representation, but it is in litigation that such conflicts occur most dramatically, and it is in

64

litigation that lawyers confront head-on the central questions about their role: What are my responsibilities to clients, courts, and opponents? To truth and justice? What effect does advocacy have on my character and values? Can I represent the "guilty"—and should I?

In the next several chapters, I will explore how Christian faith and values can shed light on these intractable problems. My goal is to help lawyers situate their work as an advocate within a broader religious frame of meaning. Or, to put it simply, to see how litigation too can be viewed as an element of the lawyer's calling.

## THE LAWYER AS HIRED GUN

In Chapter 1 I sketched what I call the standard vision of the lawyer's role. This standard vision, or Code, can be expressed in two values: *partisanship* and *neutrality*. The lawyer is a partisan who owes his undivided allegiance to his client and who does whatever it takes to achieve his client's goals. And the lawyer is neutral in the sense that he does not let his personal values or moral scruples interfere with his efforts on behalf of a client.

Partisanship and neutrality permeate all of legal practice, but they reach their zenith in the courtroom, where two adversaries square off in ritualized combat. Like the hired gun of the old west, the courtroom lawyer is the paid champion of his client. If a real-life hired gun was challenged to justify his work, he would probably shrug his shoulders and say, "I just do what I'm paid to do." Likewise, when a lawyer is challenged to defend his conduct, his usual response echoes the hired gun: "I was only doing my job. I was just representing my client."

The hired gun mentality is expressed in a famous quotation from Lord Brougham in the 1820s: "[A]n advocate, in the discharge of his duty, knows but one person in the world, and that person is his client. To save that client by all means and expedients, and at all hazards and costs to other persons, and amongst them, to himself, is his first and only duty; and in performing this duty he must not regard the alarm, the torments, the destruction which he may bring upon others. Separating the duty of a patriot from that of an advocate, he must go on reckless of the consequences, although it may be his unhappy fate to involve his country in confusion."[3]

Imagine this! A lawyer knows *no* loyalty other than to his client. He is oblivious to the "torments" and the "destruction" he causes others. This sort of thinking leads inevitably to no-holds-barred advocacy, where the courtroom becomes the O.K. Corral, and a trial a gunfight littered with the bodies of its victims.

Ironically, the epithet of the hired gun can be viewed either as the highest compliment or sharpest criticism of a lawyer. Many lawyers contend that the hired gun mentality serves as a bulwark for the protection of the weak and vulnerable. They see the lawyer as the defender of the underdog and the last-best-hope of the oppressed. For defenders of the image, the hired gun brings to mind the "macho heroics of the frontier, with the lawyer wearing the white hat"[4] and fighting courageously for his client.

For many others, however, especially critics of the profession, the hired gun metaphor expresses what is worst rather than best about the lawyers of today. To call lawyers hired guns is to accuse them of being "lackeys who are prepared to perform servile acts of immorality and lawlessness at the beckoning of paid clients." Former Supreme Court Chief Justice Warren Burger, for example, has mourned the decline of the image of the lawyer as officer of the court, a development he blames on "cynics who view the lawyer much as the 'hired gun' of the Old West."[5] For Burger, the hired gun is no hero but a black-hatted villain.

### The Wounds of the Hired Gun

Given this ambiguity, it comes as no surprise that both real benefits and serious problems result from the legal profession's infatuation with the hired gun.

The great advantage of hired gun thinking is that it instills in lawyers an unflinching loyalty to their clients. In a trial, each side must present its own case as persuasively as possible, and point out the weaknesses in its opponent's version of the facts. Only in this way will the judge and jury be able to render a fair decision that reflects the merits of the case. Each litigant, then, needs a champion who will fight for his client without trying to impose his own values on the client. The hired gun image helps ensure that lawyers will not be weak-willed partisans who abandon their clients at the first hint of trouble or dilute their loyalty because of a fear of upsetting powerful social, economic, or governmental interests.

Despite the real benefits, however, there are serious shortcomings with the hired gun metaphor. Some of the problems are systemic. There is no doubt that hired gun thinking contributes to the delay, the costs, the gameplaying, the large number of frivolous lawsuits, and the procedural abuses that plague the American legal system. As a distinguished judge has lamented: "Lawsuits now are not merely a means to resolve disputes but protracted acts of warfare. The purpose is not merely to win, but to 'chew the other guy up,' to 'nail witnesses to the cross,' to 'destroy' the opposition, to 'rearrange their anatomy.'"[6] When lawyers see themselves as hired guns, they will do anything to win.

Not surprisingly, the common perception of lawyers as the hired guns of clients contributes markedly to the public distrust and criticism of lawyers. Negative views of lawyers are tied to a perception that lawyers care only about money and will do anything for their clients without regard to right and wrong.

As troubling as the systemic costs and the costs in public esteem are the moral costs incurred by lawyers themselves. Hired gun thinking leads to an abdication of moral responsibility for our actions. The ordinary morality of everyday life—don't lie, don't cheat, don't deceive, don't hurt others if it can be avoided—no longer applies to us, we insist, and so we are free to do as a lawyer what ordinarily we would never think of doing. We feel justified in using any argument, any tactic, any legal "loophole" to advance our client's cause, without regard to the morality of ends or means. Our client's cause is transformed into a kind of idol to which we give our absolute devotion.

In short, living as a hired gun obligates the lawyer to *compartmentalize* his life, to cordon off his work from the rest of his life. He deludes himself into believing that what he does at the office bears no relation to his moral and religious values.

Such an attitude makes it easy to lose sight of the consequences of our actions. We forget that it is not some impersonal pie-in-the-sky abstraction (not a "plaintiff" or a "defendant," not a "client" or an "adversary") but real people who are often helped but sometimes hurt by our actions. People lose their homes, exhaust their bank accounts, sometimes end up in jail or dead because of the work of lawyers. This is not to deny the good and important work that lawyers do but only to insist that the work has moral consequences, and therefore carries with it moral responsibilities.

It is not easy to live a compartmentalized life. Lawyer Wayne Brazil, looking back over his life as a litigator, recounts the moral and psychological costs that lawyers pay for their single-minded win-at-all-costs mentality.[7] Brazil found himself manipulating people and information to serve his clients' interests. Money and winning became his primary motivators.

Over time Brazil discovered that it was impossible to cordon off his work from the rest of his life. He warns: "[T]here is a very real danger that the modes of behavior that began as adaptations to a special professional setting will gradually expand to fill virtually all of the lawyer's interpersonal space. Subtly, we may come to view all persons as proper for manipulation and become suspicious that all people will manipulate us if the opportunity and need arises."[8]

The suspicion, the amorality, the game-playing can spread like a virus, infecting relations with family and friends. In the end, the attempt at compartmentalization self-destructs, and the lawyer can find himself treating even his loved ones as adversaries out to take advantage of him.

The problems with the hired gun image are serious enough to demand a reconsideration of its privileged place in the profession. It does capture a part of what it means to be a lawyer (loyalty and devotion to clients are important), but only a part. It is a half-truth "masquerading as the whole truth."[9]

### Beyond the Hired Gun

For all lawyers, it would make sense to count the costs of living as a hired gun. But for Christian lawyers, the task is even more imperative. In terms of the language of Chapter 1, Christian lawyers who adopt the hired gun mentality succumb either to the model of *Christ in Harmony with the Code* (they see no tension between their work and their Christian values, and adopt the hired gun mindset without reservation), or the model of *Christ in Tension with the Code* (they are aware of the possible conflict between their work and religious values, but they split their life between home and work, functioning at work in accord with the hired gun image).

As I discussed earlier, however, neither of these models is adequate for the Christian lawyer. The hired gun's compartmentalization of life is contrary to the gospel truth that all of life is sacred and under God's sovereign rule. It sits uncomfortably with the Christian calling toward love, justice, and discipleship. The gospel has a lot to say about self-sacrifice and forgiveness of enemies but not much about the manipulation and complete destruction of opponents! It is not possible to reconcile the hired gun's abdication of moral responsibility with the Christian's obligation to act responsibly toward his neighbors and his God. A *Transformist Model* of lawyering demands more of lawyers— and promises more in return.

Let us consider, then, a different approach, a different model, more suitable for the Christian lawyer who professes that his faith and his religious values should permeate all of life, even his work as an advocate.

### THE LAWYER AS HEALER AND PEACEMAKER

If the hired gun is only one way to envision the lawyer, then the challenge facing the legal profession—and especially the Christian lawyer—is to explore other images and metaphors that can preserve the important values served by traditional imagery while liberating lawyers from the morally impoverished world of the hired gun. What these new images might be is not clear, but lawyers have a rich reservoir at their disposal. After all, lawyers are not only criticized as hired guns, mouthpieces, and ambulance chasers; they are also praised as public servants, counselors-at-law, and officers of the court.[10] Each of these images has its own implications for the way lawyers see themselves and their work.

Although there are a number of images that deserve attention, I want to focus on the idea of the lawyer as *healer* or *peacemaker*. Former Supreme Court Chief Justice Warren Burger, who as we saw above is a strong critic of the hired gun, proposes an alternative vision of the lawyer: "The entire legal profession—lawyers, judges, law teachers— has become so mesmerized with the stimulation of the courtroom contest that we tend to forget that we ought to be healers—healers of conflicts. Doctors, in spite of astronomical medical costs, still retain a high degree of public confidence because they are perceived as healers. Should lawyers not be healers? Healers, not warriors? Healers, not procurers? Healers, not hired guns?"[11]

A peacemaker, not a warrior. A healer, not a hired gun. This call to reconciliation and peacemaking echoes the gospel message, for Jesus taught us in his words and deeds to return good for evil, to suffer patiently, to avoid revenge, and to carry one's cross.

Indeed, Christians should be distinguished by their willingness to forgive others. As St. Paul wrote in Ephesians, "Put away from you all bitterness and wrath and anger and wrangling and slander, together with all malice, and be kind to one another, tenderhearted, forgiving one another, as God in Christ has forgiven you"(Eph 4:31-32).

We are to love one another as Christ loved us. We are liars if we claim to love God and hate our brothers and sisters (1 Jn 4:20-21). Our love is not limited to those who will love us in return but extends to our enemies as well, even to those who would drag us into court:

> You have heard that it was said, "An eye for an eye and a tooth for a tooth." But I say to you, Do not resist an evildoer. But if anyone strikes you on the right cheek, turn the other also; and if anyone wants to sue you and take your coat, give your cloak as well; and if anyone forces you to go one mile, go also the second mile....You have heard that it was said, "You shall love your neighbor and hate your enemy."

But I say to you, Love your enemies and pray for those who
persecute you…(Mt 5:38-43).

It is quite simple, really: As we forgive, we are forgiven. (Lk 6:37-
38). So it is that we pray for God to forgive us our trespasses *as we forgive others*.

Even if Christians are called to be healers and peacemakers, however, most of us do not immediately identify lawyers in this way. At
first blush, the image of the lawyer as peacemaker seems wildly out of
touch with reality. Haven't I argued that most lawyers, especially in litigation, see themselves as gunslingers who are paid to shoot first and
ask no questions?

### Law as Peacemaking

In fact, however, lawyers are peacemakers far more regularly
than most people recognize. Consider, first, the planning and counseling context. A client comes to a lawyer for help in establishing a business, selling a home, or putting her estate in order before death. The
lawyer's job is to help the client arrange her affairs to avoid legal problems before they arise. Likewise, if two parties want to arrange a business deal, their lawyers will draft an agreement that deals in advance
with possible areas of future disagreement. They will try to resolve differences peacefully through negotiation and compromise. This is a
form of peacemaking.

Perhaps a client needs assistance in complying with government
regulations. Consider a small business trying to make sense of the
bewildering multiplicity of tax regulations that could apply to a proposed investment. In this case, too, the lawyer acts as a peacemaker by
advising his client about its legal obligations and helping it to structure
its affairs to forestall later problems.

Sometimes, of course, a lawyer is employed to resolve a dispute.
Think of an argument between two neighbors about their property
line. Even here the lawyer may try to arrange a mutually acceptable
solution without resorting to legal proceedings. Perhaps the parties
can craft an agreement that is fair to both. Again, the lawyer is acting
more as a peacemaker than as a warrior.

Even if a dispute does lead to litigation, this too can be seen as a
form of peacemaking. Most studies estimate that around ninety percent of all civil and criminal cases in the United States are settled prior
to trial. This means that almost all disputes are resolved peacefully by
the parties—represented, of course, by their lawyers.

In a deeper sense, too, litigation itself is a species of peacemaking.

Law is a way to resolve disputes without recourse to self-help and vigilantism. Litigation is a substitute for violence. It lets the parties "fight it out" in the (relatively) safe confines of a courtroom. It is a quite extraordinary fact about our legal system, and one rarely noted, that unsuccessful litigants almost always accept a verdict even when they complain that it was wrong or unfair. Disappointed litigants who have had their day in court do not often resort to violence. In contrast, think of the violence that erupts whenever the social fabric of a community disintegrates into anarchy, and people feel they have no choice but to take the law into their own hands.

Lawyers, then, are peacemakers at least as much as they are hired guns, and this is true not only in the planning and counseling context but in litigation as well.

The real dominance of the hired gun image occurs at another level. While lawyers routinely function as peacemakers, they still see themselves primarily through the lens of the hired gun. Lawyers are taught in law school that they are hired guns and they think of themselves that way, even if the image is only half-true at best. The hired gun metaphor functions almost like a habit: Lawyers take it for granted, and over time it becomes a part of their self-identity.

What would it mean if legal education and practice took seriously the idea that lawyers are healers and peacemakers? Personal feelings and values would no longer be off-limits in the law school. Training in the skills of interviewing, counseling, and negotiation would become at least as important as courses in trial tactics and litigation strategies. Moral issues would be confronted openly.

Among practicing lawyers, mediation and arbitration would become the norm, and litigation would be looked upon as a last resort, almost an admission of failure (this important point is the subject of Chapter 6). The role of the lawyer would shift from no-holds-barred hired gun to committed go-between. Lawyers would no longer see themselves as "amoral technicians"[12] but as moral agents who are dedicated to resolving human conflict and who bear responsibility for the means they employ and the ends they achieve.

This last point must be stressed, for it is the single most important safeguard against the excesses of the hired gun mentality. As a Christian, dedicated to integrating my faith and my work, I cannot hide behind the role I am playing—lawyer, teacher, parent, spouse—to avoid responsibility for my actions. I am called to be a disciple of Jesus in all my actions and in all my settings. It is not a parental abstraction who disciplines my children, *I do*. It is not a theoretical spouse who lives with this woman I love and call my wife, *I do*. And it is not a lawyer who represents clients, *I do*.

There is a wonderful moment in the play *A Man for All Seasons* that expresses this well. Thomas More's closest friend, Norfolk, is pleading with him to put aside his personal scruples and sign the oath attesting to the legality of King Henry VIII's marriage to Anne Boleyn.

Norfolk is a simple man, no lawyer. He tells More to look at all the learned and wise men who support the king and have signed the oath. He asks More, "Can't you do what I did, and come with us, for fellowship?"

More replies, "And when we stand before God, and you are sent to Paradise for doing according to your conscience, and I am damned for not doing according to mine, will you come with me, for fellowship?"[13]

In the end, it is I who act and it is I who must take responsibility for my actions. Who else could it be? The Christian does not cease to be a disciple of Jesus because of the many roles he is called upon to play in life; quite to the contrary, his challenge is to bring the gospel to bear upon every aspect of his life, trusting in the power of grace to transform himself and his varied roles. This is the essence of the *Transformist Model* of lawyering.

Thus for Christians there can be no escape from personal responsibility for our actions. But if this is so, how can we make sense of the fact that lawyers sometimes represent "guilty" clients? In such a case, the lawyer seems to be nothing but a hired gun who will do anything to get his client off the hook. Given my objections to the idea of the lawyer as hired gun, can I justify the Christian lawyer representing a "guilty" client?

### DEFENDING THE GUILTY

How can a lawyer defend the "guilty"?[14] Perhaps no aspect of the lawyer's role is so poorly understood by non-lawyers or so poorly explained by lawyers. At cocktail parties and Little League games, over a cup of coffee or a glass of wine, lawyers are confronted with the accusatory question, "But how can you defend someone you know to be guilty?"

The lawyer's initial response is often to deny the accusation. I never represent the guilty, some say, because I never know if a client is guilty until the jury returns its verdict. In a sense, of course, this is true. We never know with one hundred percent certainty that a client did commit the act for which he or she is charged. No matter how strong the evidence, no matter what the client admits, there is always the possibility, no matter how slim, that the facts are not what they seem.

If lawyers must have one hundred percent certainty of a fact before they "know" it, then they never know anything. But we do not demand such a high level of certainty. The codes of professional conduct, for example, take a practical approach to the question of a lawyer's knowledge. Knowledge can be inferred from the facts. If a client says "I did it! I robbed the store," and all available evidence corroborates that admission, and there is no reason to doubt the client's word, then the lawyer can be said to have knowledge—not necessarily of the precise crime, because that depends upon the accused's mental state and upon the presence of mitigating or aggravating circumstances, but of the underlying fact that the client robbed a store.

As law professors Geoffrey Hazard and William Hodes remind us, "there comes a point when only brute rationalization, moral irresponsibility, and pure sophistry can support the contention that the lawyer does not 'know' what the situation is."[15] If a lawyer is reasonably certain of his client's guilt, is it right for him to represent the client and use his skills to win acquittal of the charges?

The usual answer rests upon a sophisticated understanding of the adversary system of justice. In a criminal case, the trial is only partially a search for truth. Certain things advocates do are meant to establish the truth—pre-trial discovery and cross examination, to name a few.

But in a criminal case, with the power of the state arrayed against the defendant, we have other goals as well. Our skepticism of unbridled state power has led us to create a complex system of rules and procedures to ensure that the state "plays by the rules." Sometimes the protection of human dignity must take precedence over the search for truth. That is why guilt must be proven beyond a reasonable doubt, why coerced confessions cannot be entered into evidence, and why our system includes the privilege against self-incrimination and the right to remain silent. If truth was the only value, we would routinely inject defendants with truth serum! Thus we claim with all seriousness that it is better for a hundred guilty people to go free than for one innocent person to be convicted.

For this reason, the lawyer who defends the guilty protects the innocent as well. As Thomas More says in *A Man for All Seasons*, "Yes, I'd give the Devil benefit of law, for my own safety's sake."[16]

A decision to plead "not guilty" is not a claim that "I didn't do it," but a claim that "Under the rules of the game, you cannot present sufficient relevant evidence to persuade a jury beyond a reasonable doubt that I did it." Law professor Jack Sammons puts it this way: A plea of not guilty forces the government to justify the harm it proposes to do to the defendant.[17] It puts the government to the "test" and gives the defendant a way to have a say in his or her own fate. Sammons asks, "How can it be wrong for lawyers to make it possible for criminal defendants to participate in his or her dispute with the government...if we believe that the government should justify the harm it intends to do to him or her?"

From this perspective, it is entirely appropriate for the criminal defense lawyer to put aside other concerns and dedicate himself unreservedly to obtaining the acquittal of his client. The lawyer may look like a hired gun, but in this way of thinking he is not a villain trampling the rights of the innocent. Rather, he is an unsung hero protecting the innocent (and sometimes the guilty) against the power of the state and the tyranny of public opinion.

I do not claim that this secular line of reasoning is wrong. It is true that defense lawyers play an important role in protecting human liberty. It is true that by defending the guilty they are also defending the innocent. For too many lawyers, however, this line of reasoning can become a comforting excuse for an anything-goes hired-gun mentality. It can tempt lawyers into supposing that whatever they do for their clients is justified by their role in our adversary system of justice.

For the Christian lawyer, the traditional justification for defending the guilty is not so much wrong as it is incomplete. There is no talk here of healing, reconciliation, or forgiveness. There is no recognition that this lawyer and this client are children of God with covenantal responsibilities to and for each other. There is no awareness that the gospel might call lawyers to something more or different than the adversary system envisions.

## THE LAWYER AS COMPANION OF THE GUILTY

A different perspective on the representation of the guilty is offered by law professor Thomas Shaffer. For Shaffer, the question whether a lawyer can represent the guilty should be approached in light of the life and teachings of Jesus: "The problem of whether to serve the guilty is answered with stories of Jesus having lunch with tax collectors and choosing his friends from among prostitutes, thieves, violent revolutionaries, and Samaritans—'many bad characters,' Matthew says (9:10)."[18]

Here is the beginning of a distinctively Christian approach to the question of defending the guilty. Christian discipleship is not so much a matter of learning rules and principles but of following Jesus. By attending to the gospel stories of Jesus, we learn the kind of journey we are called to embark on—a journey of renunciation and sacrifice. As Jesus says, "If any want to become my followers, let them deny themselves and take up their cross and follow me"(Mk 8:34). The reign of God which Jesus proclaims and embodies is marked not by power and domination, but by service and dispossession.[19]

The path of following Jesus is a hard one, a path most of us would just as soon avoid. It means standing as Jesus did with the poor and the outcast. It means stripping away the delusion that we are somehow "better" than others or "nearer" to God. It means humility rather than prideful self-importance:

> You know that among the Gentiles those whom they recognize as their rulers lord it over them, and their great ones are tyrants over them. But it is not so among you; but whoever wishes to become great among you must be your servant, and whoever wishes to be first among you must be slave to all. For the Son of Man came not to be served but to serve, and to give his life [as] a ransom for many (Mk 10:42-45).

If we are called to serve the lowly and the outcast, who could need our help more than the accused in a criminal trial? As Shaffer puts it, lawyers do not so much "represent" the guilty as *minister to the guilty*. We are not so much advocates as companions. "If the three crosses on Calvary mean anything, they mean that no one is so repulsive, or so condemned, that he is not entitled to have a companion in his misery, and that none of us—not even the Son of God—is too good to be chosen as the companion."[20]

Everyone, even the guilty criminal—especially the guilty criminal!—needs a companion, a friend, someone to stand with him and for him. My covenant obligations call me to be faithful to my client and not abandon him, to be there for him, and to put his interests before my own. Jesus, after all, died for the guilty—I am called only to serve the guilty.

Shaffer, therefore, approaches the problem of defending the guilty from the opposite direction of most secular writers on the subject. For him, the interesting question is not: How can a lawyer defend the guilty? The real question for the follower of Jesus is: How come we don't serve the guilty more often and more willingly? Why don't we see that as integral to our ministry of Christian lawyering?[21]

William Stringfellow, a well-known Christian theologian and lawyer, struggled with this question of how to reconcile his Christian values and his work as a lawyer. He concluded that his work as an advocate could be an expression of "the freedom in Christ to undertake the cause of another (including causes deemed 'hopeless'), to intercede for the need of another (without evaluating it, but just because the need is apparent), to become vulnerable (even unto death) in the place of another."[22]

To intercede for another without stopping to question, but simply because the person is in need—this is the calling of the Christian, any Christian, but a calling that Christian lawyers have a special responsibility and opportunity to fulfill in their daily work.

Brian Peterson, a criminal attorney, writing in the *Christian Legal Society Quarterly*, expresses a similar vision of the lawyer's role.[23] Why should a Christian bother with criminal defense work? Why not leave it to someone else? Peterson finds the answer in the story of Jesus. Like Jesus, we are called to "preach good news to the poor...to proclaim release to the captives...to set at liberty those who are oppressed."[24]

Peterson notes that for most criminal defendants, the criminal act itself is the tip of the iceberg, beneath which are more basic emotional, economic, and spiritual problems. If the lawyer can develop a relationship of trust with the defendant, forging a true covenant, it is possible that some of these deeper issues may be addressed. For the accused, there is great value simply in having a single friend who does not condemn him. Perhaps the lawyer can speak a prophetic word to help the defendant come to grips with and take responsibility for his actions. Perhaps the lawyer can help the defendant visualize a future different than his past. The covenantal relationship between lawyer and client may become an avenue of grace and healing for the accused—and for the lawyer as well, who may find his own biases, preconceptions, and comfortable middle-class values challenged by his encounter with the accused.

Although some offenders—the truly dangerous—must be imprisoned, Peterson notes that for many others imprisonment is a waste of resources and lives. Too often no one in the legal system explores alternatives to prison. No one thinks beyond the question of guilt or innocence. Here is a task for the criminal defense lawyer.

Indeed, it is often said that ninety percent or more of those charged with a crime are guilty of breaking the law. At the same time, ninety percent of all cases are disposed of without trial. Only rarely does a lawyer argue successfully to a jury that a "guilty" defendant should go free. The reality of the criminal justice system is that most of the time the lawyer's job is to advocate for the accused with respect to punishment and sentencing rather than guilt or innocence. The lawyer is not trying to "get the defendant off" but trying to work within the system to bring the punishment in line with the crime and to seek, if possible, an atmosphere that may lead to rehabilitation rather than what Peterson calls "reverse evolution—turning man or woman into beast."[25]

The defense lawyer can speak for the defendant—not necessarily in the courtroom, not even most importantly there—but within the bureaucratic morass of the legal system, where no one else has the defendant's interests truly at heart. The defense lawyer's job is to force the system to acknowledge that the defendant is not just a social misfit, or a statistic, or a criminal, but a human being with hopes and dreams and fears. A human being who, like any of us, stands in need of repentance and redemption.

From this perspective, the defense lawyer is more than a hired gun. The lawyer is a friend for those who have no friends, a companion for those who are alone and afraid. The lawyer has an opportunity to mirror Jesus' love and be an instrument of forgiveness and healing for the accused. By doing so, he ministers to Christ as well, for we serve our God by serving each other.

The question for the Christian lawyer is not, "How can you work to get a guilty person off?" The real question is "Will you stand by this person, this flawed and sinful human being, and speak a word in his behalf?"

## THE LAWYER'S OBLIGATION TO THE TRUTH

My son, watching the O.J. Simpson trial at school, came home perplexed. He had watched the legal wranglings of prosecutors and defense lawyers as they argued for over an hour about the internal operating procedures of the Los Angeles police department. "What does that have to do with whether or not he's guilty?" my son asked.

Even if there are good reasons—secular and religious—why lawyers can represent the "guilty," it does not follow that everything a lawyer does on behalf of his client is justified. My son's naive question cuts to the heart of the matter: Do lawyers have an obligation to the *truth* as well as to clients?

A lawyer who imagines himself as a hired gun does not worry about whether his actions contribute to or detract from the truth. He is confident that if he presents his case as forcefully as possible, and his opponent does the same, then, in the clash of half-truths, truth will appear. Furthermore, he realizes that truth is not the only value that the legal system serves. Protecting human rights and the dignity of the defendant is sometimes more important.

There is a good deal of truth in this, and yet can anyone really deny that the purpose of a trial—not the only purpose, to be sure, but a primary one—is to find out what happened and apportion blame accordingly? Certainly our legal system's legitimacy depends in large part on the public perception that truth *will* emerge from the courtroom testing of opposing views. Ask someone on the street, a non-lawyer, what a criminal trial is about, and the answer will be something like, "To determine if the defendant is guilty. To find out if he really did it." If we knew for certain that the adversary system did a poor job of ascertaining the truth, wouldn't we be motivated to reform it? Isn't "justice," albeit a hard word to define, a matter of *results* as well as *procedures*?

Yet it seems as if much of what a lawyer does is calculated not to serve the truth but to obscure it. Lawyers routinely twist and distort evidence, so the criticism goes. They hide documents, speak half-truths, cross-examine truthful witnesses to make them look like liars, use delay and legal "technicalities" to defeat a legitimate claim—the litany of supposed vices goes on and on.

If we keep in mind the values a trial serves—the discovery of truth and the protection of human dignity—we can construct a rough guideline for lawyers: *The lawyer's actions on behalf of clients should facilitate the search for truth and the protection of human dignity.* Conversely, a lawyer should avoid actions that make it more difficult to arrive at the truth or that threaten human dignity.

The great legal philosopher Lon Fuller, writing with John Randall, argued for a similar approach by advocates: "The advocate plays his role well when zeal for his client's cause promotes a wise and informed decision of the case. He plays his role badly, and trespasses against the obligations of professional responsibility, when his desire to win leads him to muddy the waters of decision, when, instead of lending a needed perspective to the controversy, he distorts and obscures its true nature....Thus, partisan advocacy is a form of public service so long as it aids the process of adjudication; it ceases to be when it hinders that process, when it misleads, distorts and obfuscates, when it renders the task of the deciding tribunal not easier, but more difficult."[26]

A lawyer does his job well when he helps the decision-maker arrive at the truth: when he makes arguments forcefully, challenges his opponent's assertions, introduces evidence the other side has ignored, probes the stories of witnesses to test their memory and credibility. On the other hand, a lawyer dishonors his role when he suppresses evidence, misrepresents the facts, or tries to wear down the other side by frivolous delaying tactics. A lawyer should not take advantage of procedural rules that were designed to further the truth in order to frustrate their purpose.

This perspective gives lawyers a kind of moral rudder in litigation, but it does not solve all the problems that can arise. Especially difficult are issues that involve a possible clash between the search for truth and the protection of a client's human dignity.

### Client Perjury and the Lawyer

A good illustration is the current debate about client perjury. Although the law forbids perjury and forbids lawyers from covering it up, many judges claim that perjury is pervasive and on the rise.[27] What if you know (recall that "knowledge" does not mean one hundred percent certainty) that your client is going to lie upon the stand?

Some prominent lawyers and law professors take the view that a lawyer in such cases should seek to discourage the client from lying but, if the client insists, should put the client on the stand, question him as usual, and keep confidential the fact of the lie. This is necessary, they argue, for the lawyer-client relationship to flourish. A lawyer cannot serve effectively as an advocate without establishing a relationship of trust with his client. The client must feel free to reveal everything to his lawyer—the good and the bad, the exculpatory and the incriminatory. A lawyer should not violate this sacred trust by revealing the secrets of his client.

This image of the lawyer-client relationship bears a superficial resemblance to the notion of covenant that I proposed earlier. In actuality, though, it transforms a covenant into a conspiracy. The idea of covenant does *not* mean that a lawyer must put aside his own values and morals when representing a client. Fidelity to covenant does not mean "I'll support you in whatever you do," as the Israelites found out in their dealings with God and as we know from our daily relations with friends and family. As I pointed out in Chapter 4, a lawyer's prophetic ministry to clients includes a willingness to challenge the client and even to say "no" rather than abandon his own moral values.

A client's essential goodness is not respected by abetting him in whatever he does, regardless of the moral consequences, but by holding before him an image of the kind of person he can be, by the grace of God. A lawyer helps his client by encouraging him to be the best, not the worst, he is capable of being.

Nor does the lawyer respect himself as a creature of God if he covers up the perjury. To do so is to abandon moral responsibility for his actions. How can he reconcile this with the rest of his life? How can he hope to integrate his faith and his work when he is, quite literally, living a lie?

Then there is the lawyer's duty to the truth to consider. By joining in the lie, the lawyer subverts the core values of the judicial process. He does not aid the judge and jury in their task of rendering an informed decision, but makes their task more difficult. "Perjury strikes at the heart of our system," says one prominent litigator. "When people lie in court, it undermines the whole process."[28] When a lawyer remains silent in the face of perjury, he betrays the very system of justice he has sworn to uphold.

If the lawyer and client have already forged a covenantal relationship of mutual trust and respect, the lawyer will probably be able to persuade his client to refrain from lying. But if this is not possible, and if the client surprises the lawyer with an obvious lie, the lawyer's obligations to truth and human dignity obligate him to counsel his client to come forward and admit the lie. If the client will not do so, the lawyer may have to reveal the falsehood.

Lawyers, I have insisted, are healers and peacemakers, not hired guns. But the lawyer's duty to the truth is inseparable from his commitment to peacemaking. True peace cannot be constructed on falsehoods. The first step toward real healing is to acknowledge the way things are. Reconciliation demands honesty. I do no service to my clients by lying for them or by covering up their lies. They deserve more than that. So do I.

# CHAPTER 6

## *Lawyers and Litigation*

------------◆------------

A relative of mine periodically sends me newspaper articles about lawyers and litigation. The stories are not complimentary. Many involve lawsuits over trivial matters. I have a clipping about a claim brought by a burglar against a homeowner—apparently the burglar tripped while being chased from the house, suffered a broken ankle, and turned around and sued his victim. There's a story about two neighbors who spent a dozen years and hundreds of thousands of dollars in legal fees fighting over a few feet of disputed property. Another article recounts the thousands of dollars sought by a customer at a fast food restaurant who found an insect in his sandwich—the plaintiff claimed that he suffered not an upset stomach, as you might expect, but severe psychological trauma, nightmares, and recurring flashbacks.

My relative's stories are faintly humorous, but they raise a serious point. Most students of the American legal system complain about the increase in litigation over the last several decades.[1] Our courts are too congested, goes the criticism. Too many frivolous lawsuits are choking the system. In many parts of the country, it takes four or five years for a case to get to trial. Delay drives up costs: Judge Rudolph Gerber estimates that taxpayers are spending two billion dollars a year processing lawsuits, and in many cases the cost of processing far exceeds the value of the lawsuit.[2] Even when claimants are successful, the bulk of their recovery often goes to paying legal fees and costs.

My relative apparently believes that the guilty culprits behind the litigation "explosion" are greedy and unscrupulous lawyers quick to sue over any real or imagined injury that might garner them a hefty fee. I would not be surprised if individual lawyers sometimes encourage frivolous lawsuits, just as I suspect that some mechanics overcharge for automobile repairs, and some hospitals pad their bills when insurance is picking up the tab.

What is more interesting, however, are the underlying reasons why more and more people are turning to the legal system to resolve their disputes with each other. They do so because they feel that there is nowhere else to turn. As former Chief Justice Warren Burger puts it:

"One reason our courts have become overburdened is that Americans are increasingly turning to the courts for relief from a range of personal distresses and anxieties. Remedies for personal wrongs that were once considered the responsibility of institutions other than the courts are now boldly asserted as legal 'entitlements.' The courts have been expected to fill the void created by the decline of church, family, and neighborhood unity."[3]

Benjamin Sells offers a psychological rationale that complements Justice Burger's critique. According to Sells, people sue when they encounter some sort of intolerable problem that they believe cannot be resolved any other way. They lack the means to handle the problem on their own, so they turn to an "expert," a lawyer, who takes control of the matter and promises to deal with it for them. The rise in litigation over the last few decades suggests a concomitant decline in individual capacity or willingness to deal with the complexities of modern life.[4] From this vantage point, a lawsuit almost by definition is an admission of our personal and social failings. If only people weren't so isolated, or got along better, or took more responsibility for their lives, litigation would be unnecessary.

There are theological reasons as well to be wary of litigation. As we discussed in the last chapter, Christians are called to be a people marked by self-sacrifice and forgiveness, and Christian lawyers should see themselves as peacemakers rather than quick-draw gunslingers. If Christian lawyers are peacemakers, however, what should be their attitude toward litigation? How should they counsel clients who want to go to court? Under what circumstances should they resort to a lawsuit? These are the kinds of questions I address in this chapter.

I fear, however, that litigation is subject to so much criticism these days, and its abuses so well-chronicled, that it is easy to ignore the other side of the equation. Like most things in this world, litigation can be used for good or for ill. Let us begin by briefly considering some of the *positive* values litigation serves, values that my newspaper-clipping relative and other detractors of the legal system often overlook.

## TWO CHEERS FOR LAWSUITS

At a conference on the secular and sacred dimensions of lawyering, a practicing lawyer got up and complained that there was too much emphasis being given to the negative consequences of litigation. Too much criticism of lawsuits. "I represent abused and battered women," said the lawyer, "and let me tell you, I don't think it's such a bad thing to go to court. My clients have nowhere else to turn. The courts are their only protection."

This lawyer reminds us that litigation can often be the only means available to achieve justice. A qualified woman is turned down for a promotion because of her gender. An infant is badly burnt by a defective appliance. A credit-worthy black man is denied a home loan because of the neighborhood where he resides. A company ignores safety precautions and dumps toxic waste into a nearby stream.

Litigation is often our last best hope to uphold and vindicate important public values. Certain fundamental rights expressed in our Constitution and laws remain only a dream unless enforced by the courts. The vision of a society that treats all persons equally without regard to the color of their skin—that dream is not yet fully realized, to be sure, but no one can deny the pivotal role that lawyers and courts have played in defending and extending the rights of minorities. Where would we be without decisions such as *Brown v. Board of Education*, or lawyers like Thurgood Marshall?

In terms of the language of an earlier chapter, litigation can be a form of *prophetic ministry*. Lawyers, I have argued, have a prophetic call to work for justice, which includes an obligation to assist the weak and the needy. A lawsuit can be an instrument to compel those in power to accept their obligations to the less fortunate—to force the government, for example, to meet its legal and moral responsibilities to the poor and disabled. Recall the words of Abraham Heschel: A prophet is someone who pleads for the helpless, who is an advocate for those too weak to speak for themselves.[5]

Critics of litigation sometimes place so much weight on peacemaking and reconciliation that they forget: Peace comes at a price. The price may be continued injustice. A decision by a client and lawyer not to bring a lawsuit may only reinforce the present unjust state of affairs. But an unfair peace, a peace that merely covers over a dispute about fundamental values, is no real peace. Sometimes what is needed is an authoritative public expression of social policy that will bind not only the litigants but the wider community as well. A lasting, authentic peace presupposes justice. "If you want Peace," wrote Pope Paul VI, "work for Justice."[6]

This suggests that the criticism of litigation (and lawyers for bringing unnecessary and frivolous lawsuits) should be directed at lawsuits involving private disputes (two neighbors quarreling over their property line, for example) rather than at disputes concerning important public values. That may be true, but we should not forget the important values served by litigation even in cases involving a private dispute between two parties. As we discussed in the last chapter, a lawsuit is a substitute for violence. A judicial proceeding gives the parties the opportunity to have their day in court and present their side of the story. Judicial resolution lets the parties move beyond a dispute, put it in the past, and get on with their lives.

Litigation, then, is not an unmitigated evil, but can serve important values. The real issue for lawyers and clients is to decide *when* and under *what circumstances* it is appropriate to invoke the machinery of state to resolve a dispute.

## ST. PAUL ON LITIGATION

The place to begin is with St. Paul's first letter to the Corinthians, in which he addresses the issue of Christians suing each other in secular, pagan courts. Paul writes:

> When one of you has a grievance against another, do you dare to take it to court before the unrighteous instead of taking it before the saints? Do you not know that the saints will judge the world? And if the world is to be judged by you, are you incompetent to try trivial cases? Do you not know that we are to judge angels—to say nothing of ordinary matters? If you have ordinary cases, then, [why] do you appoint as judges those who have no standing in the church? I say this to your shame. Can it be that there is no one among you wise enough to decide between one believer and another, but a believer goes to court against a believer—and before unbelievers at that?
>
> In fact, to have lawsuits at all with one another is already a defeat for you. Why not rather be wronged? Why not rather be defrauded? But you yourselves wrong and defraud—and believers at that (1 Cor 6:1-8).[7]

This passage can be read several ways. Some Christians interpret it to bar all lawsuits by Christians, others read it to prohibit all lawsuits between Christians.[8] The ex-lawyer I met in divinity school, who told me "a Christian can't be a lawyer" (see Chapter 1), in effect adopted the first interpretation and extended it another step: If Christians should not bring lawsuits, they should not bring them on behalf of other people either, and therefore they should not become lawyers!

My own method of interpreting scripture is not so literal. I believe that we must take into account the time and the context in which Paul was writing. Paul's letter was addressed to a particular community at Corinth that was torn by conflict and division. At the time, Christians were a tiny minority in the pagan Roman empire. Christian values had no influence on the secular courts. In our own time, things are different, with most members of society professing to be Christian, with our laws based (at least in part) on Christian values, and with the legal system itself populated by Christian lawyers and judges. The simple *us versus them* mentality of Paul's era has grown considerably more complex today. I am reluctant to take Paul's words as establishing some sort of absolute prohibition on litigation effective against Christians in all times and places.

Does that mean that Paul's words have no meaning for us today? Are we free to ignore them and go blithely on our way, suing each other without hesitation, using litigation as a weapon of revenge to beat the other side into submission? The answer is *no*! There is a way to take Paul's words seriously if not literally, to move beyond the particular problem he faced at Corinth and to extract a more general perspective on litigation that is relevant to Christian lawyers and clients here and now.

At its core, Paul's letter to the Corinthians lays down two basic principles to govern the church. First, Paul takes a strong *pro-mediation* view and says that Christians should seek to resolve their disputes with each other internally within the church, rather than taking the issues to secular law courts. He stresses the value of community at a time when the church was a small, despised element in society. Second, Paul adopts an *anti-litigation* approach and insists that it would be better for Christians to suffer wrongdoing rather than go to court to vindicate their rights.[9] As law professor Robert Taylor puts it, "In other words, the rule of law for a Christian, so to speak, is not to push forward one's rights, but voluntarily to renounce those rights and personally to absorb any and all injuries that otherwise would be amenable to legal remedy and redress."[10]

As a starting point, then, Christians should be reluctant to bring a lawsuit, and should support community-based alternatives to litigation, such as mediation. This is consistent with the stress on reconciliation and renunciation of rights that is at the core of the gospel. In the Sermon on the Mount, Jesus explicitly preached against using the courts to remedy injustice. "If anyone sues you and takes your coat," said Jesus, "let him have your cloak as well" (Mt 5:39-43).

Not only the teachings of Jesus, but his life as well, should give pause to anyone contemplating resort to the judicial system. When falsely accused of crime, Jesus did not fight back, retaliate, or seek revenge. As Professor Taylor wryly notes, "It does give one ample pause for reflection to imagine our Lord surrounded by a bevy of attaché case–carrying attorneys zealously trying to procure from Rome and the Sanhedrin every legal remedy, if any, to which the Crucified One arguably would have been entitled."[11]

Among Christian thinkers, it is probably John Calvin who offers the most thoughtful interpretation of Paul's teaching in 1 Corinthians. Calvin's reading of 1 Corinthians deserves our careful attention, for he combines a commitment to reconciliation with an acute sensitivity to the psychological and spiritual costs of litigation.

## JOHN CALVIN ON LITIGATION

It is easy to forget that Calvin was a lawyer before he was a systematic theologian. Although he soon left behind a career in the law, his legal training and familiarity with the law are evident in his treatment of 1 Corinthians 6.[12]

Calvin's reading of the passage is something of a compromise between two extreme views that he rejects. On the one hand, Calvin opposes those who believe that Christians owe no allegiance to secular magistrates and are not permitted to make use of the civil law system. To the contrary, Calvin insists that the magistrates are ordained by God for human benefit. Christians are free to call upon them and their courts for assistance and in return owe them a duty of obedience.

At the other extreme, Calvin is responding to those who "boil with a rage for litigation." This group is never satisfied unless they are quarreling with others. "[T]hey carry on their lawsuits with bitter and deadly hatred, and an insane passion to revenge and hurt, and they pursue them with implacable obstinacy even to the ruin of their adversaries." Note the uncanny resemblance to modern trials which often degenerate into no-holds-barred battles between warriors in three-piece suits.

Calvin's response to these extreme views is to declare that lawsuits are permissible—but only if they are used rightly. This applies both to plaintiffs and defendants. The plaintiff who feels aggrieved should seek justice but should have no hatred or passion for revenge. It is better to suffer a wrong than be consumed by enmity. Likewise, a defendant should litigate without bitterness and solely with the desire to defend what is his or hers by right.

Calvin's primary worry is that litigants will be so carried away with anger and revenge that Christian love will be impaired. When this happens, even the just cause becomes unjust. For Calvin, nothing—not even the pursuit of legal justice in a courtroom—can be allowed to impair the ties of love and fellowship that bind Christians to each other: "[A] lawsuit, however just, can never be rightly prosecuted by any man, unless he treats his adversary with the same love and good will as if the business under controversy were already amicably settled and composed."

How many of today's clients could meet such an exacting standard? How many lawyers?

When Calvin turns to Paul's condemnation of lawsuits, he argues that Paul was not barring resort to the courts in all circumstances. Paul himself taught that the magistrates and courts are ordained by God for human benefit. Indeed, Paul did not hesitate to call upon the secular courts when he was unfairly accused of violating the law, even going so far as to demand his right as a Roman citizen to call upon Caesar himself for a judgment (Acts 21:28).

For these reasons, Calvin concludes that Paul was not laying down an absolute rule against all litigation but was condemning the greed, anger, and hostility that plagued the church at Corinth. According to Calvin, "Paul inveighs against that mad lust to go to law, not simply against all controversies." The Christian is free to use the legal system as long as he does not crave revenge for real or imagined wrongs. The key is to focus on the *inner disposition* of the litigant. If the Christian can proceed without resentment or vengeance, a lawsuit can be prosecuted: "[I]t is not out of order for Christians to pursue their rights with moderation, so long as no damage is done to love."

The critical question, then and now, is whether it is possible for a litigant and lawyer to engage in a lawsuit with moderation and love toward an adversary. For those of us who have spent any time around courts and litigants, a great deal of skepticism is in order. Is it really possible to bring a lawsuit and not be infected by the mad lust for revenge?

Calvin, trained as a lawyer, has no illusions about the likelihood of Christian forbearance, and he identifies a number of vices that are likely to motivate or accompany a lawsuit, including greed, impatience, revenge, hostility, anger, and obstinacy.[13] Underlying these particular vices is the more fundamental failure to heed the words of Jesus and bear wrongs patiently, respond to evil with kindness, love our enemies, and pray for those who persecute us. Litigation tempts good people to behave badly.

Calvin comes perilously close to conceding that lawsuits are unavoidably evil, yet he wants to leave some room for Christians to make use of the legal system. His solution is a masterful example of subtle, nuanced thinking, lawyerly in the best sense of the word. His awareness of the psychological, moral, and spiritual costs of litigation, and his reading of St. Paul, lead Calvin to adopt a *presumption*—to use the legal language, which seems fitting—against litigation. In general, Christians are to settle their disputes within the community of faith and bear their wrongs patiently without retaliation. Resort to the courts is allowed only in the *exceptional case* when it can be undertaken without impairing Christian love and the ties that bind the community of believers. Everything hinges on the disposition of the litigant. "In all this," says Calvin, "love will be the best guide."

In short, reconciliation and forgiveness must take priority over the vindication of abstract rights.

Before considering the implications of Calvin's views for modern Christian lawyers and litigants, it would be helpful to examine a contemporary critique of litigation that supplements and indeed supports the thrust of Calvin's thinking. This is the view that litigation is a species of violence that runs counter to the gospel and should therefore be restrained as much as possible in a violent world.

## LITIGATION AS VIOLENCE

I explained earlier how litigation can be a form of peacemaking, a substitute for violence. That is true, but it is only part of the truth. As we have also seen, a trial is a form of combat in which great harm can be done to lawyers, litigants, and third parties. Professor Robert Taylor calls a trial a form of "regulated warfare."[14] His comment brings to mind the work of the late law professor Robert Cover who proclaimed the unpleasant truth that the legal system is a form of legalized violence.[15] Cover insisted that the most important thing about judges— and, by implication, lawyers as well—is not what they say but what they do: "The judges deal pain and death." Whatever the justifications, violence and coercion underlie any legal system: "A judge articulates her understanding of a text, and as a result, someone loses his freedom, his property, his children, even his life. Interpretations in law also constitute justification for violence which has already occurred or which is about to occur. When interpreters have finished their work, they frequently leave behind victims whose lives have been torn apart by these organized, social practices of violence."

Professor Taylor suggests that there are at least three levels to the institutionalized violence of a lawsuit.[16] First, litigation is premised upon the idea that persuasion and moral dialogue are impossible; instead, litigation is "a fight unto death in which irreparable harm (economic, psychological, and spiritual) is done to parties."

Second, in order to assure impartiality and due process, the parties to a lawsuit are stripped of what makes them who they are, their character and personality—their very God-given uniqueness. In litigation, the "human being is regarded as a skeleton with rights hanging from its limbs like ornaments from a Christmas tree." Litigants are treated not so much as persons but as abstractions or objects.

Third, litigation is violent because it seeks to right a wrong by doing another wrong. By focusing on restoring the plaintiff to wholeness, litigation ignores the economic and other harm done to the defendant and to innocent third-parties.

If, as Cover and Taylor insist, litigation is a species of state-sanctioned violence, then perhaps it would be wise to consider the teachings of the Christian church on another type of violence: warfare. Over the centuries, Christians have attempted to limit the plague of war by constructing a number of rigorous conditions that must be met before it is morally permissible to undertake armed conflict. This body of thought is known as the *just war* doctrine. A look at the criteria for a just war provides insight into the conditions under which it is permissible for Christian clients and lawyers to undertake a lawsuit with its attendant violence.

## LITIGATION AND THE JUST WAR

Just war theory begins with a bias against the use of force similar to Calvin's presumption against litigation: Christians are expected to love their enemies and avoid harm to others. In some cases, however—for example, an attack by an aggressor on an innocent victim—the command not to harm others is in tension with the obligation to love our neighbors, protect the innocent, and restrain evil.[17] The just war doctrine is an effort to establish a workable balance between these conflicting values.

There are several criteria that must be met before a war can be deemed just. If we examine them in light of their relevance to litigation, we can begin to identify the prerequisites to a "just lawsuit."

### Just Cause

War is permissible only for a good reason—for example, to defend the innocent or protect human rights. Wars of retribution are morally impermissible. In the same way, Christians should not go to court unless they have serious and important reasons for doing so. Greed or revenge are not sufficient. The Christian lawyer has the obligation to explore frankly the motives that impel her client to seek legal redress.

## Competent Authority

The decision to go to war must be made by those entrusted by the public with the responsibility, not by private individuals or groups. Congress, for example, is given the constitutional authority to make war. Likewise, the decision to go to court cannot be made by the lawyer alone; nor can the lawyer merely acquiesce in a client's ill-considered choice to file a lawsuit. The decision to file a lawsuit must be made jointly. Each of the partners must be free to raise her concerns or doubts about the contemplated lawsuit.

## Probability of Success

It is wrong to undertake hostilities when the situation is hopeless and the resort to force has no chance of success. In the same way, lawyers should ask whether there is any realistic hope of success if they embark upon a lawsuit. Is a lawsuit merely a futile gesture? Is the client's real purpose merely to harass the other side? If so, litigation should not be commenced (and filing the lawsuit may expose the client and the lawyer to legal sanctions).

## Proportionality and Discrimination

War is so destructive that it should not be undertaken lightly even if the "right" is on our side. We must still ask: Do our rights and values justify war with its accompanying violence, suffering, and death? The harm to be inflicted must be proportionate to the good expected to be achieved. This is the principle of *proportionality*. The principle of *discrimination* is a necessary corollary: It is never morally permissible to make a deliberate attack on innocents and non-combatants. As much as possible, attacks must be directed at military targets, not civilians.

Similarly, a person may have legitimate reasons for going to court but should first consider whether the potential gain to be achieved justifies the pain and expense that are likely to follow. The lawyer's role is to help the client appreciate the goals that might realistically be achieved and the costs that will likely be incurred.

The costs of a lawsuit are not limited to the consequences for the client. A lawsuit is a crude and unwieldy weapon that cuts broadly and can do a great deal of harm to opponents and to third parties (think for a moment of the children buffeted and battered by their parents' divorce). The lawyer has an obligation to take reasonable steps to minimize the harm done to opponents and third-parties (I will return to this important issue in Chapter 7).

## *Last Resort*

War cannot be justified until all peaceful alternatives have been exhausted. Even when war commences, efforts at peace must continue. Likewise, litigation should be undertaken only after other alternatives have been tried and found wanting. At times it may not be possible to persuade the other side to engage in alternatives to litigation, such as negotiations or informal mediation. It may take the filing of a lawsuit to open the other's eyes to the seriousness of the dispute and the legitimacy of your client's cause. But the duty to seek reconciliation does not end when the lawsuit begins. Experienced lawyers know that the parties' interest in settling a case usually increases as the time until trial dwindles. It is never too soon or too late to consider settling a case.

As we can see, there are striking parallels between the church's just war doctrine and the type of analysis that should guide a lawyer and client contemplating litigation. But how should a lawyer and client determine whether a lawsuit is warranted *in this case*? How should the lawyer counsel her client? What kinds of questions should she raise?

### THE LAWYER'S ROLE

An example will help. Consider a case in which my client is injured slightly in an auto accident. The other driver was clearly at fault. My client's expenses are covered by insurance, but there is the possibility of bringing a lawsuit and perhaps recovering a windfall. Should my client sue?

As a starting point, it is entirely appropriate to look behind the narrow legal issue—can we sue the other driver for negligence?—and explore the larger context of the dispute and the likely consequences of going to court.

A number of questions should be considered: Did my client suffer a wrong? If so, how serious? Does it warrant resort to the clumsy machinery of the state? How likely is it that we will prevail if we do file suit?

What does my client really want—is it a question of money, respect, or wounded pride? A certain amount of anger and bitterness at the other driver is natural, and the lawyer should give her client ample opportunity to express those feelings openly. But revenge is a poor reason for a lawsuit and is ultimately self-destructive—is that what motivates my client, or is there some important value here that cannot be achieved in any way other than through the courts?

It is also important to help the client realize that a lawsuit is a poor vehicle for dealing with the underlying causes of a conflict. If two parties start a company and later have a falling out, litigation may be able to recompense the "innocent" party, but it cannot restore the bonds of affection and loyalty that have been shattered. Indeed, as Calvin recognized four hundred years ago, a lawsuit almost always exacerbates the hurt feelings, selfishness, anger, and greed that lie below the surface of the disagreement. In our hypothetical case of the auto accident, perhaps what my client really needs is not money or legal vindication but a simple apology, an acknowledgement of her suffering, and a sense of being respected as a person.

Does my client appreciate the costs of litigation? Not just the financial costs, or the costs in time and worry and sleepless nights, although these are real costs that should be considered. But the other costs as well. What effect will the months and years of legal wrangling have on her emotional and spiritual life? What effect will it have on her image of herself? It is not paternalistic to confront a client with the likely consequences of litigation and remind her that the "victor" in a trial is often like a punch-drunk boxer left standing when the bell sounds, only to collapse from exhaustion a moment later.

What about the costs to others—does it make any difference, for example, that the other driver has a large family and little money, and will be financially destroyed by a sizable judgment against him? Is the good my client hopes to achieve proportionate to the harm that will be inflicted?

These are the sorts of questions that a lawyer and client should explore before making the decision to bring a lawsuit. No one gains if the client rushes heedlessly into litigation, and it is the lawyer's responsibility to provide the time and information—the "breathing space"— necessary to make a wise decision. To do so the lawyer must be honest about the real-world consequences of going to court. (It may even be the case that the lawyer believes, after a full and frank discussion, that there are insufficient reasons to go to court. If the client insists on bringing a lawsuit, the lawyer may have to decline to participate and the client may have to seek legal counsel elsewhere.)

It was Abraham Lincoln who expressed the lawyer's role best when he counseled, "Discourage litigation. Persuade your neighbors to compromise whenever you can. Point out to them how the nominal winner is often the real loser—in fees, expenses, and waste of time. As a peacemaker, the lawyer has a superior opportunity of being a good man. Never stir up litigation. A worse man can scarcely be found than one who does this."[18]

The kind of wide-ranging dialogue between lawyers and clients that I envision can only become a reality if the parties create an atmosphere of trust and respect. Only then will the lawyer feel free to talk honestly about the pros and cons of litigation. Only then will she be able to approach her role as a peacemaker and healer of human conflict rather than a hired gun. This, in turn, brings us back to the importance of lawyers and clients forging a covenantal relationship between equals. Everything depends upon that crucial first step.[19]

## ALTERNATIVES TO LITIGATION

In his first letter to the Corinthians, St. Paul not only criticized Christians for taking their disputes to pagan courts, he also urged them to establish mechanisms within the church to resolve disagreements among their members.

Most Christians today do not look to the church as the primary vehicle for settling disputes with their fellow Christians. But Paul's stress on the value of community still has much to say to us. As I suggested earlier, litigation is often an admission of our lack of community, and it can serve to drive people farther apart rather than bring them together. Given this result, Christians, and especially Christian lawyers, should be in the forefront of exploring creative options for resolving disputes that will not fracture the bonds of love and community that unite all Christians and all persons.

Perhaps the most fruitful path to explore is what is commonly known as alternative dispute resolution, or ADR, which seeks to settle disputes not by a courtroom battle but through mediation, arbitration, and negotiation. Usually, supporters of ADR emphasize its savings in time and money, and the way it focuses less on winning than on maintaining relationships.

At the same time, St. Paul's teaching in 1 Corinthians and John Calvin's critique of litigation are quite consistent with the overall thrust of the movement, and provide a theological rationale for ADR. ADR is preferable to litigation not only because it saves time and money, although it does both, but also because it fosters reconciliation rather than retaliation, community rather than competition. It encourages forgiveness rather than revenge, and emphasizes the ties that bind human beings rather than the differences that divide them. In all this, it is the mirror image of litigation.

ADR is a young movement, but already its effects are being felt. The blossoming of mediation centers around the country, the wide-spread use of ADR for minor civil claims, the efforts to encourage media-tion in divorce and child custody disputes, the training of lawyers and non-lawyers to serve as arbitrators and mediators—all these are efforts to establish workable alternatives to litigation.

Furthermore, some evangelical Christians have taken Paul's words to heart and have begun to establish Christian conciliation centers to which Christians can bring their disputes with each other to obtain a non-legal remedy.[20] These centers rest upon the scriptural underpinnings of 1 Corinthians and Matthew 18, a passage where Jesus sets down guidelines for imposing discipline within the church.[21] Their goal is clearly reconciliation rather than legal vindication: "The purpose of Christian conciliation is to glorify God by helping people to resolve dis-putes in a conciliatory rather than an adversarial manner. In addition to facilitating the resolution of substantive issues, Christian conciliation seeks to reconcile those who have been alienated by conflict and to help them learn how to change their attitudes and behavior to avoid similar conflicts in the future."[22]

Christian lawyers should be among the leaders in efforts like these. They should lobby their local and state bar associations to fund programs in ADR. They should seriously consider becoming trained as mediators and arbitrators. Some may wish to explore the explicitly Christian roots of ADR and join the movement to establish religiously-based conciliation centers.

Most importantly, Christian lawyers should make ADR a routine part of their legal practice. Whenever they are involved in an actual or contemplated lawsuit, they should actively explore with clients and opponents the possibility of settling the dispute through ADR, whether formal (via a court-sponsored program) or informal (through the inter-vention of a trusted third-party). Not all cases can or should be resolved through ADR, of course, but the Christian lawyer who sees herself as a healer, not a hired gun, will look upon ADR as the rule rather than the exception.

Let us give the last word on this issue to Supreme Court Justice Antonin Scalia. In commenting upon 1 Corinthians 6, Justice Scalia expresses the general sentiments that should guide Christians: "I think this passage has something to say about the proper Christian attitude toward civil litigation. Paul says that the mediation of a mutual friend, such as the parish priest, should be sought before parties run off to the law courts....I think we are too ready today to seek vindication or vengeance through adversary proceedings rather than peace through mediation....Good Christians, just as they are slow to anger, should be slow to sue."[23] This is good advice for Christians—and for Christian lawyers, too.

# CHAPTER 7

## *Toward an Ethic of Care*

———————◆———————

Several of my friends and acquaintances have undergone painful divorces. At the outset, most are confident they can resist the pressures toward hostility and bitterness. Often they believe quite sincerely that their divorce will be different.

"We're not going to get involved in name-calling," they promise. "We've already settled everything. There's not much for the lawyers to do. We're going to stay friends."

These are laudable intentions, but they almost always prove to be delusions. No matter how hard the parties try, no matter how many issues they thought they had resolved, once a divorce petition is filed and the adversary system begins to grind out justice, there is a near-irresistible drift into all-out-warfare. Too often good intentions go out the window, as homes, cars, even children become bargaining chips, weapons to beat the other side into submission. No one emerges unscathed—not the "winner," not the "loser," and certainly not the innocent children.

In a divorce action as in any lawsuit, a lawyer is expected to serve as the zealous advocate of her client. But are there any limits to her advocacy? Must a trial inevitably degenerate into a gunfight?

Last chapter I explored the decision to file a lawsuit. Assume now that after giving due weight to the teachings of St. Paul and Calvin, a lawyer and client have jointly decided that a lawsuit (or the defense of a lawsuit) is necessary to right a wrong that cannot be remedied in any other way. Our aim now is to examine the role of the Christian lawyer *during* the prosecution of a claim. In the midst of a lawsuit, how do I balance my duties to my client with my calling to love my enemies and work for reconciliation? Can an advocate be a peacemaker, too?

We can start by calling to mind Calvin's admonition about the proper disposition that should accompany a lawsuit. The parties should litigate without bitterness. The test Calvin lays down is not an easy one: "[I]t is not out of order for Christians to pursue their rights with moderation, so long as no damage is done to love."[1]

*So long as no damage is done to love.* A lawsuit can be brought if and only if it can be prosecuted without impairing Christian love. If anger, bitterness, or the lust for revenge infects a lawsuit, even a just cause becomes unjust.

Lawyers are in a unique position to guard against the perversion of the legal process into an instrument of resentment and revenge. I have already argued that a lawyer should engage her client in a moral dialogue in which the parties jointly participate in making important decisions such as whether to bring a lawsuit or not. This moral dialogue should continue throughout the life of a lawsuit. The lawyer's responsibility to bring her moral and religious values to her work does not cease when she has concluded, after exploring the matter fully with her client, that a lawsuit is warranted by the facts of the case. The lawyer remains responsible for her own actions and, with her client, remains jointly responsible for the conduct of the lawsuit. The duty to help a client "count the costs" of litigation does not end the instant the lawsuit begins.

Therefore, the lawyer has a *personal* moral obligation not to let a lawsuit degenerate into bitterness and revenge. If she refuses to play petty games of harassment, for example, and declines to project all the evil in the world upon her opponent, then her client will be more likely to accept something less than the complete and utter destruction of the other party.

At the same time, the lawyer should work to defuse the anger and bitterness of her client (to do so, of course, she must first encourage her client to air those feelings and come to terms with them). Even though a lawsuit can sometimes be justified, it is still a form of violence, and the lawyer should try to restrain its force, not give it full rein to devastate the lives of litigants, lawyers, and third-persons.

This is a difficult idea for many lawyers to comprehend. They may understand the need to discuss fully with their client the question *whether* to sue, but once a case is filed, and the litigation process begins, they have their eyes fixed on one goal: winning at all costs. My friends who have undergone divorces report that their lawyers rarely if ever suggested ways to reduce tensions or curb hostilities. The lawyers fueled the flames of resentment and anger when they might have snuffed out the fire.

This is perhaps the most important lesson for lawyers in litigation. They control the tempo of the litigation; they control its tone and its feel. They decide how nasty it will become.

An example illustrates this point. A distinguished older lawyer in my hometown told me of a case he litigated involving business partners who had experienced a falling out. Their business venture collapsed when one party wrongly expended about five thousand dollars on a purchase without informing the other. This lawyer represented the plaintiff. At first his client merely wanted an accounting of the money and his fair share of the company's assets. But as the lawsuit progressed, with each side filing motions, deposing the other, submitting interrogatories and the like, the stakes rose inexorably, until the plaintiff wanted to destroy his former partner in retaliation for all the wrongs he felt had been inflicted upon him.

Eventually the battle escalated to the point that the client was willing to spend far more money than it was worth in order to have the personal satisfaction of imposing pain upon his former partner—at which time the lawyer took him aside and said, "Look at what this trial is doing to you! You're a good person but now you've got the blood lust and you've lost all sense of judgment! What you're doing isn't right!" Finally, the lawyer was able to persuade his client to settle the case for a fair price.

This is part of the lawyer's job, too, what I earlier termed the lawyer's *prophetic ministry*. Not to dictate to the client, but to call the client back to his or her better self, to remind the client of what is truly important, to help the client see that even in the midst of a lawsuit, reconciliation is possible.

## LITIGATION ETHICS

I have argued that lawyers should not engage in litigation tactics that frustrate or distort the search for truth, such as covering up a client's perjury. Lawyers often argue, however, that it is impossible to maintain high ethical standards during a lawsuit. You may not want to play "hardball," but if the other side does, you feel no choice but to respond in turn, lest your opponent gain some sort of tactical advantage by resorting to "dirty tricks." This worry contributes to the game-playing, procedural abuses, delay, harassment, and kill-or-be-killed mentality that plagues present-day litigation. Good and decent lawyers find themselves doing things they would never do in ordinary life—all in the name of zeal on behalf of the client. This has an effect not only on the legal system but on lawyers as well. As we have seen, the suspicion, manipulation, and aggressiveness that lawyers cultivate at work can end up distorting their character and their relationships outside of the office as well.

There are several things that can be said in response to the claim that everybody-does-it-so-I-have-no-choice. First, it may be a cliché but it is no less true that we should strive to treat others the way we would like to be treated. The golden rule is only one formulation of this essential foundation of the moral life. There may be times when I will need to counter an opponent's tactical abuses, but the decision to respond is a moral decision, and I should be clear about that. Jesus said that we are to do unto others as we would have them do unto us, not as we *fear* they *might do* unto us.

Furthermore, if I let my opponent's tactics dictate my response, I overlook the possibility that my own conduct can set the tone for our relationship. Perhaps if I act honestly and fairly, my opponent will respond in kind. Someone must have the courage to take the first step.

We should not be too quick to dismiss the basic decency of our opponent or discount the moral authority we possess. A lawyer friend of mine reports that early in a lawsuit, before the parties have begun a downward ethical spiral, he often telephones the opposing counsel and says, "I'd like us to agree on some basic rules of the game that will assure fairness to our clients without forcing either of us to engage in false displays of macho heroics or Rambo-like tactics. What do you say?"

There are also ways to counter the tactical abuses of opponents without resorting to them ourselves. Federal and state rules of procedure, and the codes of professional responsibility, place limits on the zeal of advocates and establish mechanisms to combat trial tactics used solely to delay or harass the other side. We should explore such judicial and professional remedies before we conclude that since our opponent is engaged in slimy tactics we have no choice but to reciprocate.

We must remember that these are not matters for the lawyer alone to decide. It is the client's case, and together the lawyer and client are engaged in a joint venture. It is true that tactical decisions such as how to structure an argument, or what questions to ask a witness, are within the lawyer's domain of special competence. But decisions about how hard to fight or about how much harm to inflict upon the other side are not simply tactical questions but implicate the client's overall vision of what the lawsuit is about and what it is meant to accomplish. These decisions should be made jointly.

Indeed, it would not be out of place for a lawyer to raise such issues in the very first meeting with a client, to say in effect, "If we agree that I will represent you, I will fight hard for you and I will do my best to advance your cause. But there are some things I won't do for you or for anyone else: I won't lie, cheat, or misuse the legal process.

I'm sure you wouldn't want me to do any of those things, but I want you to know that my own values prohibit me from acting that way."

Rather than driving prospective clients out the door, I suspect that an honest airing of moral values would be attractive to many clients. In each of the cities I have lived, there have been a number of lawyers who were well-known for their exemplary moral character, even in the heat of a trial. In each case, these lawyers were respected by their peers and highly successful.

In the end, the best check upon the excesses of litigation is not the rules of the profession or even judicial oversight but the values and character of individual lawyers. The Christian lawyer is a zealous advocate, to be sure, but at the same time she recognizes her obligations to the legal system and to other persons. She is committed to pursuing the legal rights of her clients in a way that will preserve relationships and minimize the harm to others. As a peacemaker, she seeks to balance *rights* with *caring*.

## RIGHTS AND CARING

At the risk of some simplification, there are two fundamental moral orientations that lawyers consciously or—more likely—unconsciously adopt in their practice of law. Some lawyers follow what I call an *ethic of rights*, and others are more likely to adopt an *ethic of care*.[2]

This is the conclusion of Rand and Dana Crowley Jack, who, in their book *Moral Vision and Professional Decisions*,[3] discuss the results of their interviews with several dozen practicing lawyers. Their work builds upon an important distinction among developmental psychologists. Some psychologists, often identified with Lawrence Kohlberg, envision moral development as a hierarchical progression culminating in a commitment to individual rights and justice. A second group, associated with Carol Gilligan and her pioneering study, *In a Different Voice*,[4] holds up the centrality of caring for the moral life.

In their research, Jack and Jack discovered that while some lawyers conceive of the moral life primarily as a matter of following the rules of the game embodied in the adversary system and the codes of professional responsibility, others are more concerned with minimizing harm and preserving relationships. While an ethic of rights stresses competition, the ethic of care emphasizes cooperation; instead of rights, responsibilities; instead of formal and abstract thinking, contextual reasoning; instead of the fair resolution of disputes, the avoidance of harm.

Consistent with the findings of Gilligan, Jack and Jack found that women were more likely to stress caring, while men stress rights, although they caution that nearly everyone adopts both orientations to some extent. Rather than seeing the two approaches as mutually exclusive, we should consider them as points along a spectrum, with individual lawyers inclined more to one pole or the other.

The contrast between these moral perspectives can be illustrated with an example from Jack and Jack's research. In one of their hypothetical cases, they asked lawyers to imagine that they were representing a client in a divorce action.[5] The client is seeking custody of the two children from the marriage. In the course of the representation, the lawyer inadvertently discovers that the client represents a risk of serious harm to the children. The information is not known and will never be known by the other side unless the lawyer reveals it. If the information is not revealed, the lawyer's client will win the custody battle; if the information becomes known, the other side will probably prevail. There is no doubt in the lawyer's mind that the other party is the superior parent who deserves custody of the children.

What should the lawyer do? Jack and Jack found that some lawyers emphasized their role as zealous partisans whose moral obligations were to their client alone. One male lawyer described his dilemma as follows: "Well, it's not a moral issue for me, it's a legal issue for me....On the one hand I've got a client privilege to protect, and on the other hand, the law says that I've got the best interests of the child to protect. I mean it's not even a moral issue anymore. It becomes a legal issue what to do in the circumstances. You've got two competing issues...I guess most of the time things are falling in favor of the fact that I have an ethical and legal responsibility to my client, and that's the position I take."

This lawyer adopts an ethic of rights. He frames the issues narrowly in terms of *his client's* privileges and rights, and he refuses to consider the consequences for the children. He sees himself as an advocate and nothing else.

In contrast, a female lawyer responded in the language of care: "Well, the moral issue is I don't want to participate in increasing the hazard to a child; the ethical issue is whether you perpetrate fraud on the court. And I find that I can resolve the two very well together. I mean, it's not money we're taking about here. We're talking about people, and you can't undo it. When you're talking about money and maybe it's damages, people will sort it out and pick it up and go on; they can redo. You can't undo an incidence of violence. You can't undo something like that for a child. You can't undo what's going to happen for the rest of children's lives."

This lawyer tries to balance her duty to her client with her responsibility toward the children. The terrible consequences for the children—you can't undo an incidence of violence—provide a focus for her thinking. She raises questions that the ethic of rights ignores: Who will be hurt? How seriously will they be hurt? What will be the effect on the people and their relationships?[6] Unlike the first lawyer, the second lawyer's approach is contextual—she "burrows into the specifics of the situation,"[7] the real nitty-gritty of the problem, and does not take refuge in her role as an advocate or in the rules of the adversary system.

Rights-oriented lawyers naturally gravitate toward the hired gun model that I described earlier, while care-oriented lawyers are more likely to see themselves as healers and peacemakers. Although I have criticized the hired gun mentality, I acknowledge that rights-thinking serves important values. A commitment to rights is the hallmark of an adversary system of justice. The very language we use to express the goals of the system highlight this rights-orientation—we demand "equal justice," follow "due process of law," and insist that ours is a system of "laws not of men." As Jack and Jack correctly observe, "the premises of the legal system closely parallel those of the morality of rights. Both share concern for fairness, equality, procedural regularity, integrity of rules, and the duty to prevent interference with autonomous others."[8]

The problem with rights-thinking is that, taken to an extreme, it ignores other essential dimensions of the moral life. Those who stress rights and rules can easily forget that the actions of lawyers have *consequences* for real people in the real world. People lose their money, their freedom, and sometimes even their lives because of what lawyers do. It is too easy for a rights-oriented lawyer to allow his entire moral universe to be bounded by the interests of his client, thereby losing sight of his own accountability for his actions.

Lawyers need to bring a wider context to their work, one which does not deny their fundamental commitments to clients, but which locates those commitments in a web of other relationships that matter as well. In this way, they can temper the excesses of the hired gun mentality with a commitment to reconciliation, even in the midst of a trial. This wider context can be illustrated by an examination of a famous trial from scripture—the story of a king, two harlots, one baby, and a very sharp sword.

## KING SOLOMON AND THE HARLOTS

The story of Solomon and the two harlots presents in condensed form the paradigm of all litigation: two advocates arguing before a single impartial judge (1 Kgs 3:16-28). The very structure of the story calls to mind a judicial proceeding. First the women present their cases, and then Solomon issues his judgment.[9]

The outline of the story is familiar to everyone. Two unnamed harlots come before Solomon for judgment. The first woman tells her story. "We share the same house," she says. "I gave birth to a child when this other woman was there. Three days later she gave birth. During the night her child died. She took my baby from me and put the dead baby alongside me. When I awoke in the morning, I found the corpse, but when I looked at him closely, I realized that it was not my child."

The second woman immediately snaps back, "No, the dead child is yours. Mine is the living one." The first woman counters, "No, the living child is mine and the dead child is yours." The two women argue back and forth like the best (or worst) of lawyers.

Solomon has a problem. There are no witnesses who can be called to corroborate the testimony of either woman. When he finally speaks, it is as if he is scratching his head and wondering aloud. All he can do is repeat the words of the women. "This woman says 'my son is alive and yours is dead,' and the other says, 'your son is dead and mine is alive.'" By repeating the woman's words, he underscores the impossibility of reaching a solution through an assessment of their conflicting stories.

Instead, he calls for a sword, saying, "Cut the child in two and give half to one woman and half to the other." Apparently, there is no way to resolve the deadlock except by resort to violence and the brute power of the judicial office. (We might see Solomon's call for a sword as a gross caricature of the violence inherent in all litigation.)

But this is certainly not the meaning that the writer of the story meant to convey. To the writer of 1 Kings, where our story appears, Solomon was the wisest of all kings, whose wisdom was demonstrated by the extraordinary way he untangled the mystery of the infant's parentage.

A more-plausible reading of Solomon's actions is presented by biblical scholar Phyllis Trible. As Trible explains, this is a story of two women locked in a terrible struggle for power, lacking the means to free themselves from their dilemma. Solomon takes neither woman's side in the contest. Instead, by calling for a sword, "the king moves to break this egoistic and dualistic thinking—mine versus yours—by showing its ultimate absurdity."[10]

Now, in the moment of crisis, the women reveal their true character by their response to Solomon's command. There is no longer any need for a judge, for the two women judge themselves.[11]

The first woman, moved with love for her son, cries out, "Please, my lord, let her have the child—do not kill him!" Swayed by compassion, she is willing to surrender her rights in order to save the child. Love overrides self-interest. Not so the other woman. She insists, "It shall not be yours or mine. Divide it in two!" She demands mathematical "fairness" even though the result would be monstrously unfair. She wants her share regardless of the cost in human life. In her twisted logic, half a child is better than none!

Only now does Solomon announce his judgment. "Give the first woman the child, for she is his mother." By forcing the dispute to its absurd and deadly end, Solomon has awakened from the first woman a loving compassion that was always there but was concealed by the formal trappings of the legal proceedings. We cannot be absolutely certain that the first woman is the biological mother, but we know without a doubt that she is the better mother.[12] As the story ends, Solomon turns over the baby to the first woman, and all Israel marvels at his wisdom.

### Integrating Rights and Caring

What does this familiar story have to say to Christian lawyers engaged in litigation?

Let me suggest one reading. The story of Solomon teaches that loyalty to clients and pursuit of legal rights, no matter how laudable, can degenerate into a cruel legalism, unless balanced by a concern for preserving relationships and minimizing harm. Rights must be complemented by caring.

From this perspective, the second woman illustrates what can result when the pursuit of rights is not mitigated by a concern for the persons affected by our actions. She is like the lawyer who will do anything, and hurt anyone, to win a case.

In sharp contrast, the first woman demonstrates a commitment to both rights and caring. If she had no concern for her rights under the law, she would never have come before the king to plead her case. Yet if she cared only for her own rights and interests, she would have become a moral monster like the second woman. She too would have claimed that half a child is better than none. Instead, as Carol Gilligan observes, this is a woman who understands that an ethics of rights must be tempered by a concern for persons lest it degenerate into a "blind willingness to sacrifice people to truth."[13] She is interested less in abstractions such as "truth" and "fairness" than in the concrete costs of her actions. She knows when to assert rights and argue her case, but she also knows when to let go of her rights and stop arguing. Determining the real mother is important, but it is not the most important thing: *It is more important that the baby live!*

Finally, there is Solomon, the most ambiguous of the characters. He barely acknowledges the presence of the two women who stand before him and evinces no compassion for them in their predicament. Faced with an unsolvable dilemma, he calls for a sword. Yet it is Solomon's call for a sword that reveals the absurdity of an unqualified devotion to rights at the expense of relationships. Only a madman or a monster would wield a sword against a baby, but a person of uncommon wisdom might call for a sword to force the moment to its crisis, confident that in that moment the legal masks would slip away and the naked character of the litigants stand revealed. Solomon is possessed of the wisdom of God not so much because his fertile mind concocts a clever stratagem to resolve an impossible dilemma, but because beneath his veneer of detachment he knows how to evoke the love and compassion of the mother. In this he is a model lawyer and a model judge.

## *Justice as Procedures and Outcomes*

We might put it this way: Lawyers in general see justice as mostly a matter of *procedures*, of due process, of impartial rules impersonally applied. As long as fair rules are fairly applied, they do not concern themselves much with the consequences of their actions or whether the result is objectively "true" or "fair."

But the mother in the Solomon story was equally concerned about *outcomes*—who would be hurt and who would be helped. She would have understood the profound wisdom of a remark by Judge John Noonan: "Abandonment of the rules produces monsters; so does neglect of persons."[14]

The Christian lawyer abandons neither. She is an advocate for her client, but she never forgets the costs of her actions. She strives for reconciliation even when pursuing a client's interests. She knows that justice entails a concern for *both* procedures and outcomes.

Lawyers, we know, have special covenantal obligations to clients, but at the same time they are joined in a larger, more-inclusive covenant with all people, including adversaries. As Joseph Allen reminds us, "From a Christian standpoint the whole of humanity is to be understood as one covenant community."[15] Our special obligations to clients should not blind us to the fundamental unity of all persons. When a young *lawyer* approached Jesus and asked "Who is my neighbor?" Jesus responded with the parable of the good Samaritan, teaching that our neighbor is anyone and everyone in need of our help (Lk 10:29-37).

Return for a moment to the example from Jack and Jack in which the lawyer in a divorce action discovers that the other party is a better parent of the children. An ethic of rights says, in effect, "My loyalty is to my client alone." An ethic of care considers the consequences for the children and attempts to balance those with the obligations of zealousness. It places a value not only on winning but on protecting the children from harm.

Notice that the first approach gives a simple answer. It lets the lawyer know precisely what to do: fight for his client, regardless of his knowledge that the client is abusing the children. It has the advantage of clarity and objectivity.

In contrast, the second approach provides less certainty. Perhaps the lawyer could encourage her client to get counseling. Perhaps—if she has the kind of deep covenantal relationship with the client that I have espoused—she might even ask, "Do you think it would be best for your children to live with you? Do you really want to expose them to possible harm?" Perhaps she might support, or at least not oppose, the appointment of a guardian to represent the best interests of the children.

Perhaps…there are no easy answers here. An ethic of care is by its very nature contextual, situational, and embedded in the complexity of everyday life.

Consider another example. You represent a landlord who is seeking to evict a tenant for non-payment of rent. You learn that the tenant has failed to make her payments because her husband recently left her, and she has been forced at age fifty to find a paying job after years of working at home. The only job she can get pays little more than minimum wage. When the divorce goes through in six months, however, the woman stands to gain a modest sum of money, which should make her living situation more secure. You know that she is hard-working and responsible, and you suspect that over time she will rise in her company and command a better wage.

Your client wants to get rid of the tenant and re-lease the apartment. This raises no particular "ethical" issues under the professional codes of conduct. Of course, you can evict the woman! Your client seeks nothing more than what the law guarantees. Under an ethic of rights, your job is to achieve that objective.

Yet to say that you can legally obtain an eviction order is not the same as saying it is the right thing to do. An ethic of care encourages you to look beyond what you *can* do and begin to ask what you *should* do. It broadens the moral landscape to encompass the results of the lawsuit on the tenant. This might lead you to find out as much as you can, legally and ethically, about the tenant's situation and prospects. You might suggest to your client some alternatives to an eviction proceeding—for example, reducing the rent for the present and then increasing it after the divorce settlement. In an extreme case, an ethic of care might even lead you to refuse to represent the landlord if you are convinced (after a full and frank dialogue) that he is intent on causing needless harm and suffering to the tenant.[16] The choice of clients, after all, is a moral decision too.

Litigation is a fight, but it need not be a fight to the death. It should be conducted with a serious appreciation of the consequences of our actions on others, including third-parties (the children from the divorce hypothetical) and even adversaries (the tenant behind on her rent). We are called to love our neighbors and our enemies. To be zealous advocates, while seeking to preserve relationships and minimize harm. Even when we draw our guns for a client, we need not shoot to kill.

## LOVE AND JUSTICE

We can conclude this discussion of rights and caring by comparing the contemporary notion of justice with the biblical understanding. As the Roman Catholic bishops of the United States put it: "Biblical justice is more comprehensive then subsequent philosophical definitions. It is not concerned with a strict definition of rights and duties, but with the rightness of the human condition before God and within society. Nor is justice opposed to love; rather, it is both a manifestation of love and a condition for love to grow. Because God loves Israel, [God] rescues them from oppression and summons them to be a people that 'does justice' and loves kindness. The quest for justice arises from loving gratitude for the saving acts of God and manifests itself in wholehearted love of God and neighbor."[17]

This intimate connection between love and justice is particularly evident in the writings of the Hebrew prophets. Hosea says, "Sow for yourselves justice, reap the fruit of steadfast love" (Hos 10:12).[18] Micah proclaims, "[God] has told you, O mortal, what is good; and what does the Lord require of you but to do justice, and to love kindness, and to walk humbly with your God?" (Mic 6:8).

Biblical justice thus transcends a narrow concern for rights and procedures and includes a loving concern for the other. In the Bible, the just society *is* the loving society. Justice is the instrument of love and love the root of justice.[19] Judge John Noonan makes the point well: "Justice to persons, Augustine reminds us, may be identified with love—an active service to another, who is loved."[20]

Modern lawyers too often are infected with a moral blindness that causes them to see only a part of the moral landscape. They identify justice with fair procedures, with fighting for a client, with the adversary system itself. In some ways this half-vision has proven as debilitating as no vision, for it has allowed the ethics of rights to masquerade as the whole of the moral life. When that happens, there is no room left for compassion, love, and healing.

The cure for this blindness is to remove the moral blinders. This is true for all lawyers, but especially for the Christian, who is committed to forgiveness and reconciliation, not winning-at-all-costs. A *Transformist Model* of lawyering summons Christian lawyers to find a place in their legal practice for the ethic of care alongside the prevailing ethic of rights. Only when lawyers integrate both perspectives into their work will they truly come to be both partisans and peacemakers. And only then will they come to know what the Israelites knew so well: True justice is more than a matter of rules and rights. People also matter. Caring also counts.

## A POSTSCRIPT: RECONCILIATION AS AN IMPOSSIBLE POSSIBILITY

When I share these ideas about litigation with practicing lawyers, most concede that there are far too many lawsuits filed. A good number nod in agreement when I talk of lawyers as healers rather than hired guns. Some endorse my proposals that litigation be approached as a last resort rather than a first impression, and a few even agree that rights should be balanced by caring.

Practicing lawyers, however, even if they agree with me in principle, routinely dismiss my proposals as flatly unrealistic. They claim that I have ignored the financial pressures that drive lawyers to pursue litigation. Simply put, it is not in the lawyer's financial interests to tell a client "I don't think you should sue," or to say "Look, you have a legal right to bring a lawsuit, but do you really think you should?"

Instead, lawyers tell me, it is almost always in the lawyer's interest to sue. A lawyer who charges by the hour makes more money the longer the clock is ticking. And a plaintiff's lawyer who takes a case on a contingency fee makes nothing if after deliberation her client decides not to file a lawsuit. As one lawyer sarcastically commented, "No law firm stays in business if it says no to clients."

I wonder if there is an adequate answer to such objections. It is true that lawyers face increasing pressures to recruit clients and keep them satisfied. It is true that too many lawyers are subject to the tyranny of the billable hour.

My lawyer friends may be right. They may stand to lose financially if they come to see themselves as healers of human conflict dedicated to reconciliation as much as winning. I believe they will gain far more spiritually and morally than they will lose in the bargain, but I do not deny there may be costs. The *Transformist Model* of lawyering does summon lawyers to change the way they look at clients and litigation.

None of this makes my proposals unrealistic, however, only difficult. My proposals are as realistic as real lawyers and real clients want them to be.

Another way to put this is to borrow an apt phrase from theologian Reinhold Niebuhr, and say that what I am calling for is an *impossible possibility*.[21] Niebuhr used that language when analyzing Jesus' teachings on love in the Sermon on the Mount. He conceded that it is impossible for any sinful human being to live up to the rigorous standards of the sermon. None of us will be able to practice absolute forgiveness of our enemies or total self-sacrifice. None of us can love as completely and selflessly as Jesus commands. But that does not mean that we can ignore the Sermon on the Mount, however much we would like to forget it and get on with our everyday lives. Although Jesus' ethic of total love is impossible for us to fulfill, it remains relevant to our daily life, for it always judges us, challenges us, and calls us to do more. We can always *approximate* the Sermon on the Mount more fully in our lives, even if we can never live up to it absolutely.

In the same way, my vision of the lawyer as a healer of human conflict is an ideal, a goal. I believe that it is an appropriate goal for the Christian lawyer who wants to integrate her religious values with her work as an advocate. And I believe that it is realistic—there are always things to do, opportunities to take, in order to approximate the ideal more closely. We have the choice to approach our work more as a healer or a hired gun, even if in the real and messy world of the law we will inevitably partake a bit of both.

When lawyers claim that my proposals are unrealistic, I am often at a loss for words. What can I say? Perhaps only this: As long as lawyers convince themselves that talk of healing and reconciliation is unrealistic, then it will remain an unfulfilled dream—but no more unrealistic or impossible than Jesus' own words at the Sermon on the Mount.

Ultimately, the gospel is as possible or as impossible as we choose to make it.

# CHAPTER 8

## *A Tale of Two Lawyers*

━━━━━━ ◆ ━━━━━━

I have not had a lot to say about the codes of professional responsibility that govern the work of lawyers. That is not because I deny their importance. Codes provide a measure of (more-or-less) objective guidance to lawyers, and therefore provide a means of holding lawyers accountable to courts and clients. They establish the ethical bottom-line below which a lawyer cannot fall without risking professional sanction.

Too much reliance on codes, however, can degenerate into a least-common-denominator mentality where legality is confused with morality. Furthermore, while codes can establish legal minimums, they cannot speak to the heart of the individual lawyer. They cannot empower a lawyer to be caring or courageous, which is just as much a part of the moral life—actually, quite a bit more, I suspect—than the ability to analyze the codes in good lawyerly fashion. Codes cannot identify the circumstances when zealous partisanship should give way to reconciliation. They cannot give a lawyer guidance on when and how to balance a client's legitimate interests against the harm that will be done to others. They cannot tell a lawyer whether a particular tactic that *may* be employed *should* be employed. They cannot help a lawyer decide whom to accept as a client and whom, given his deepest personal values, he should decline to represent. And they cannot provide guidance for the lawyer who is grappling with questions that the code itself ignores—questions such as the goals of lawyering, the lawyer's accountability for his actions, and the relationship between faith and work.

Instead of focusing on the codes, I want to tell the tale of two lawyers whose stories teach us something important about what it means to be a lawyer and a person of faith. One of these, Leo Tolstoy's Ivan Ilyich, is an example of a lawyer whose life went wrong. His story teaches us something about how easy it is to drift into a life of self-deceit and meaningless amorality. The other, Thomas More, is a model or paradigm for Christian lawyers because of the way he integrates his faith with his work and remains true to his deepest values. I believe that the stories of these two lawyers provide more guidance on what it means to be a Christian and a lawyer than all the codes and laws ever written by or for lawyers.

## IVAN ILYICH

Ivan Ilyich died at the age of forty-five.[1] At that time he was a respected and influential jurist, a member of Russia's Court of Justice. He had served ably in a variety of legal and administrative posts in the provinces and in St. Petersburg, the capital, before his appointment to the bench.

In law school, Ivan was already the kind of person he would remain until his death, "a capable, cheerful, good-natured, and sociable fellow, thought strict in the performance of what he considered his duty; and he considered as his duty whatever was so considered by those in authority over him." He was always attracted to those with power and status. He adopted their values, their virtues, and their vices: "As a law student he had done things which had before that seemed to him vile and at the time had made him feel disgusted with himself; but later on when he saw that such conduct was practised by people of high standing and not considered wrong by them, he came not exactly to regard those actions of his as all right but simply to forget them entirely or not be at all troubled by their recollection."

Here we confront the essential core of Ivan's character. He was not an evil man, but he was a man with little understanding of himself, without a firm center or solid sense of his own identity. He was like a sponge, absorbing the values and morals of the society around him. What high society condemned, he abhorred; what it applauded, he embraced.

After graduation from law school, Ivan took a job with the Civil Service. He made sure to dress well and comport himself with dignity. He performed his duties with competence, dispatch, and an integrity of which he could not help but feel a certain well-earned pride. As he rose in the legal bureaucracy, he treated those under him respectfully, never abusing his authority.

Ivan went to great measures to eliminate the personal and human dimensions from the law. He had no space in his job for feelings or emotion. Like the hired gun, he bracketed his personal and moral values when at work: "In the work itself—in his judicial investigations, that is—Ivan Ilyich very soon acquired the art of eliminating all considerations irrelevant to the legal aspect, and reducing even the most complicated case to a form in which the bare essentials could be presented on paper, with his own personal opinion completely excluded and, what was of paramount importance, observing all the prescribed formalities." Outside of the office, however, he was amusing, convivial, a lover of card games and drinking parties.

In all his life Ivan had always done what was expected, and he did the same when it came to marriage. He met a woman from a good family. She was attractive and owned a bit of property. Why not marry? It was not quite a matter of love, nor of social expectations, but a bit of both. Marriage was personally satisfying and socially advantageous.

The marriage did not turn out well. Ivan had expected nothing much to change. He desired to lead the same easy-going and respectable life he was accustomed to, but his wife was easily jealous and wanted him to spend more time with her. Her bad temper proved impossible to ignore. The birth of children increased tensions at home.

As his relationship with his wife deteriorated, Ivan's solution was to put more of himself into his job. He became what we would now call a workaholic, not because he loved his work so much, but because he loathed the rest of his life. Work became his refuge: "As his wife grew more irritable and exacting, so Ivan Ilyich transferred the centre of gravity of his existence from his home life to his work. He became increasingly fond of his official functions, and more ambitious than he had ever been before."

One incident illustrates his attitude toward work. Ivan had been married seventeen years when he found himself passed over for several promotions. At the same time, he was in serious financial trouble from living beyond his means. For the first time in his life, Ivan fell into a depression, finally rousing himself to go to St. Petersburg and find a better-paying job with the government. He did not care what type of work it was. He did not care what ministry he found a job in. All he cared about was one thing: He must have a job with a salary of 5000 rubles! Because of his connections and friends, his mission was successful. He got a job in the Ministry of Justice that paid what he wanted. Once again he was satisfied.

For a while, Ivan and his wife fashioned a fragile reconciliation. Ivan transferred his energies to his house and spent most of his free time selecting wallpaper and furniture, overseeing the upholstering, and searching for antiques. He spent his evenings with friends playing cards, or reading a book everyone was talking about, or attending parties. He and his wife moved in the best social circles. It was a comfortable life that might have continued indefinitely.

### Illness and Despair

One day, however, standing atop a stepladder to show a worker how he wanted a curtain hung, Ivan slipped and bruised his side. The injury soon healed, but Ivan began to experience odd and disquieting symptoms. At first it was nothing serious, a funny taste in his mouth, a pressure on the left side of his stomach. Gradually the discomfort increased. Ivan found himself growing more and more irritable. He and his wife began fighting again.

Eventually he went to a doctor, where Ivan found himself being treated precisely the way he treated people in the law courts. Everything was the same—the interminable waiting, the doctor's dignified and self-important airs, the look the doctor gave him which seemed to say "leave it to us and we'll handle everything."

All Ivan wanted to know was whether his problem was serious or not, but the doctor was more intrigued by the possibilities of this or that illness, taking into account certain symptoms, weighing one diagnosis against another. From the doctor's cryptic comments, Ivan surmised that things were bad, but when he summoned up the nerve to ask whether his condition was dangerous, he was rebuffed: "The doctor regarded him sternly over his spectacles with one eye, as though to say, 'Prisoner at the bar, if you will not keep to the questions put to you, I shall be obliged to have you removed from court.' 'I have already told you what I consider necessary and proper,' said the doctor. 'The analysis may show something more.' And the doctor bowed."

As Ivan's condition worsened, he became preoccupied with his illness—in a way, it filled up his life as his work and his card playing had done before. His days came to revolve around his symptoms and his medicines. For a short time, he would convince himself that he was getting better, but any problem at home or at work seemed to bring on a fresh attack, and every trip to the doctor seemed to confirm his fears that the illness was progressing.

Finally, he could not hide the truth from himself. "It's not a question of appendix or kidney but of life and...death." He realized that his death was not far off, and he was struck cold by the thought. "I shall be no more, then what will there be? There will be nothing." He found himself staring into the bleak chasm of despair.

Yet at the same time that he knew he was dying, he could not really grasp the idea. He tried to avoid the thought, to return to his old ways of life, to recreate the screens that had blocked out all thoughts of death in his earlier years. He told himself, "I will take up my duties again—after all, I used to live for my work." For a little while he would forget his illness, but then the pain would return. *It* alone seemed real. *It* alone controlled his life. Nothing could block *it* out. *It* penetrated all his flimsy defenses.

As his death approached, Ivan suffered most from the conspiracy of silence that his family, friends, and doctors all joined in. None of them understood what he was going through. They all pretended that he was only ill, not dying. He longed to be pitied, kissed, wept over, but no one was willing to confront his situation openly; to others his illness was nothing but "a disagreeable and rather indecent incident."

There was one exception. Gerassim, his servant, a simple peasant, made no attempt to ignore what was happening because to him death was a reality, an inescapable part of life. When Gerassim would clean Ivan's commode, Ivan would apologize, and the servant would smile, "What's a little trouble?" Gerassim did not hide his feelings: He simply felt sorry for his dying master. "We shall all of us die, so what's a little trouble?" he would say. Soon Ivan could bear to be with no one else.

One night Ivan found himself reliving in his imagination all the best experiences of his life. But everything that had seemed so pleasant at the time appeared meaningless and disgusting now. It was all worthless: his career, his marriage, his concern for money and status. "In public opinion I was going up, and all the time my life was sliding away from under my feet."

A terrible thought struck him. "What if I did not live as I should?" He immediately dismissed the idea as ridiculous! Had he not always done his duty? Had he not always been eminently upright, respectable, and successful?

His denials went on for several weeks, until the physical and mental pain became intolerable. One night, he found himself asking again, "What if my whole life has been wrong?" For the first time he admitted that his entire life had been a lie: "It struck him that those scarcely detected inclinations of his to fight against what the most highly placed people regarded as good, those scarcely noticeable impulses which he had immediately suppressed, might have been the real thing and all the rest false. And his professional duties, and his ordering of his life, and his family, and all his social and official interests might all have been false. He tried to defend it all to himself. And suddenly he realized the weakness of what he was defending. There was nothing to defend."

When Ivan saw his family and his doctor, his terrifying insight was confirmed. "In them he saw himself—all that he had lived for—and saw plainly that it was all wrong, a horrible, monstrous lie concealing both life and death."

The pain increased terribly. For three days Ivan screamed in agony as he struggled against the powerful force that was pushing him into the black hole of death. His agony was due both to being pushed into the hole and to fighting against it. "What hindered him from getting into it was his claim that his life had been good. That very justification of his life held him fast and prevented him from advancing, and caused him more agony than anything else."

On the third day, at the precise moment that his young son kissed him on the hand, Ivan felt himself falling through the black hole and catching sight of the light on the other side. He now accepted completely that his life had not been what it should have been, but he also realized that it was not too late to make it right. He felt his son kissing his hand, and felt sorry for him. He saw his wife, and felt sorry for her. He felt sorry for them all, he was overwhelmed with love and pity, he wanted to free them all from their suffering. He spoke to his wife and son, "Take him away...sorry for him...sorry for you too..." He tried to say more, tried to say "Forgive me," but the words came out garbled.

He searched for his pain and his fear of death, but they were gone. How could there be fear of death when there was no death? Instead of death, there was light.

"It is all over," someone said.

"Death is over. It is no more," he said to himself. And at that moment he died.

### TRAGEDY AND REDEMPTION

Ivan Ilyich was not a bad person. He was not cruel or vindictive. He was a lawyer and judge who did good work and was respected by his peers. On the day of his death, the newspapers undoubtedly published glowing tributes from the lawyers and judges who had worked with him. His career was, in all the usual ways, a successful one.

Yet no one can read the story of his life without the awareness that here, beneath the successes and achievements, lies a great tragedy. As we come to know Ivan, we see a man who has no real sense of who he is. What Gertrude Stein supposedly said about Oakland we could say about Ivan: *There's no there there*. He was a person with no sense of self. All his values, dreams, and goals came from outside. His actions and his thoughts were determined by the high society he wished to be a part of and emulated.

Time after time, Ivan is described by Tolstoy as "agreeable." To be agreeable is not itself a fault. Society depends upon certain unspoken bonds of civility. To be successful one must "usually 'fit' in." But Ivan's agreeableness had no purpose other than to be accepted. He cared nothing about achieving something creative or meaningful in his work, something life-affirming. He had no desire to use his legal talents to help the disenfranchised, for example, or to assure equal and impartial justice for all. No, he was an agreeable man because that was the only way to be successful, and he wanted to be successful only to be successful, for no greater purpose.

So it was that Ivan never caused any waves at work. He was always competent, dignified (another word Tolstoy frequently uses for him), a bit reserved. Since he had no strong feelings about anything, he was the quintessential "team player." He had no values of his own, so he never disagreed with his superiors or raised unsettling questions about right and wrong.

Like many lawyers, Ivan took pride in eliminating the personal dimension from the law. He reduced every case, every encounter, to the dry legal technicalities. He saw himself as a cog in a great grinding bureaucracy and, like many bureaucrats, he was only happy when there was a form to be stamped, a signature to be signed, a seal to be affixed. His own moral values—if he had any—were rigidly excluded from his work as he became the paradigmatic "amoral technician" I discussed and critiqued earlier. Ivan's goal, as Tolstoy puts it, was to "exclude everything with the sap of life in it."

It is striking that in his entire professional life, Ivan never confronted a difficult moral issue or agonized over a decision. The only time he was ever galvanized to oppose an "injustice" was when he decided he was being paid too little and rushed off to St. Petersburg to find a job, any job, that paid more money.

Occasionally, it is true, Ivan would be struck by a suspicion that he was not living his life as he should. Perhaps there was more to life than doing what society expected of him? But such glimpses of insight he ruthlessly suppressed. It was easier to proceed with his comfortable life.

Ivan's unwillingness to engage in moral reflection suggests an important point about the role of character in ethics. Ethics is as much a matter of character (who do I want to be?) as action (what should I do?). As theologian Stanley Hauerwas observes, "the kind of quandaries we confront depend on the kind of people we are and the way we have learned to construe the world through our language, habits, and feelings....The question of what I ought to *do* is actually about what I am or ought to be."[2]

Our character provides the context in which our decisions are made. In Ivan's case, his character was so shaped by external forces, by the people he met and the values he absorbed, that he did not even recognize the possibility of a moral dimension to his life or work. His eyes had been trained to ignore such issues, and so a comfortable amorality became his only morality.

There was no there there. No person, no human being with an inner life of introspection and doubt, fear and hope. Only the bureaucrat, the technician, the cog in the machine.

## Redemption

For many years I have read *The Death of Ivan Ilyich* with law students. I always ask the students, "Do you think this is a sad book?" Most answer *yes*. They see the book as a tragedy about a life misspent, a life never lived. There has been fierce debate in our class, however, about whether the ending of the book tempers the note of tragedy. Most of my students see little redemption in Ivan's last moments. It's too little too late, they say. Ivan never really changes his life, and his hard-won self-knowledge comes too late.

A smaller number, myself included, do not read the story as sheer unrelenting tragedy. To me it is not a sad book. The lesson I take from it is that redemption is always possible. Change can come. It depends not so much on changing how we *act* as changing how we *see*.

Ivan is trapped in a black hole, unable to live or to die. Yet once he can admit to himself that his life has not been good and can accept the unacceptable truth that he has not lived the way he ought to live, at that moment he is freed from the chains that hold him and is able to surrender to death. He finds release at the precise moment when he admits to himself his failures.

At that moment there is an ending, but there is also a beginning. As Ivan realizes that his life has been misspent, he also understands that it is never too late to set it right. He does this by the humblest of gestures: As he lies near death, as his son kisses his hand, he simply feels sorry for his wife, family, and even himself. He reconnects with the human condition, ending his voluntary exile in the land of the walking dead.

He realizes too that death is not the answer to life, but that on the other side of death there is something else, something more, another life, the real life to which we are called. Death is not the final word.

At the end of *The Death of Ivan Ilyich*, there are obvious echoes of another death. At his moment of death, Ivan has the strength only to mumble the words "sorry." He tries to say "forgive me," but he is too weak to get the words out—yet this does not matter, for he knows that "whoever was concerned would understand." Ivan's dying words parallel those of Jesus, who near death said, "Father, forgive them; for they do not know what they are doing" (Lk 23:34). At the moment of Ivan's death, someone says, "It is all over," which brings to mind the last words of Jesus at his death, "It is finished" (Jn 19:30).

Our lives parallel those of Jesus. Our death echoes his. His plea for forgiveness—they do not know what they do—applies not only to those who killed Jesus but to all of us who stumble and sin and misspend our lives. Ivan's plea for forgiveness is an affirmation of the forgiveness promised to us by Jesus himself.

And just as for Jesus, death is not the end of the story, so too Ivan's death leads to new life. "And death? Where is it?" wonders Ivan. His question recalls the words of St. Paul: "Death has been swallowed up in victory. Where, O death, is your victory? Where, O death, is your sting?" (1 Cor 15:54-55). Ivan's three days of agony are like Jesus' three hours on the cross, or his three days in the tomb: they are the pain and death that must be experienced and passed through if there is to be resurrection.

For us, too, the final word is one of hope, of resurrection. Redemption is possible, for Ivan Ilyich, for Joe Allegretti, for any of us, if we begin to see our lives clearly and acknowledge our failures and sinfulness, not in order to punish ourselves unmercifully, but to accept the unacceptable: that as we forgive we are forgiven. Redemption is possible. Always.

## THOMAS MORE

Robert Bolt's *A Man for All Seasons* focuses on Thomas More's refusal to support King Henry VIII's bid to assert control over the Christian church in England.[3] In the character of More we encounter an authentic Christian legal hero, and by following his journey through life to death we learn something about what it means to be both a Christian and a lawyer.

The author makes it clear from the outset that he is interested in the risks of losing one's self in one's work and social roles. In modern society, says Bolt, when we ask ourselves "what am I?" we tend to answer by describing ourselves more as a *thing* than as a moral agent: "'This man here is a qualified surveyor, employed but with a view to partnership; this car he is driving has six cylinders and is almost new; he's doing all right; his opinions...' and so on, describing ourselves to ourselves in terms more appropriate to somebody seen through a window. We think of ourselves in the third person."

Here is the problem: We think of ourselves in the third person, as a thing, an "it," a lawyer or a father or a spouse, rather than as a unique human being who fulfills many roles but is larger than any of them.

A good example is Master Cromwell. When someone asks Cromwell how he would like to be introduced, he responds "Well, I suppose you would call me 'The King's Ear'....It's a useful organ, the ear. But in fact it's even simpler than that. When the King wants something done, I do it."

Most of the characters in the play are like Cromwell. Their values, their morals, their principles all come from the "outside." Like Ivan Ilyich, they are sponges soaking up the culture around them. They are like lawyers whose sense of moral obligation comes not from themselves and their conscience but from what others tell them—their profession, their client, their codes of conduct.

For people like this, the highest aim in life is to fit in. To stay out of trouble. And so it is that each and every one of More's colleagues signs the oath attesting to the legality of Henry's divorce from his first wife and remarriage to Anne Boleyn. Their personal scruples notwithstanding, they know which way the wind is blowing.

There is a lesson here for those of us who are trying to integrate our religious and professional lives. One of the great temptations for lawyers is to see ourselves in the third person, as the mere instrument of our client. If we do so, of course, moral issues disappear because we compartmentalize our lives and relegate our moral and religious values to the private realm of family and friends. There is never any risk of having to say "no" to a client or the system because only a moral agent, an *I*, can stand for something—a lawyer in the third person has nothing to stand up for or against.

We see in Thomas More someone who was willing to be an I, to see himself in the first person. More knew that what he said and did mattered, that his soul was implicated in his work. While the precise issue—the taking of an oath—may seem quaint and far-fetched to us, the larger question of what we stand for and whom we owe allegiance to is as contemporary as this morning's deposition or opinion letter.

## A Sense of Self

What made More different? What gave him the strength to stand alone? It is his sense of who he is. Bolt explains: "At any rate, Thomas More, as I wrote about him, became for me a man with an adamantine sense of his own self. He knew where he began and left off, what area of himself he could yield to the encroachments of his enemies, and what to the encroachments of those he loved. It was a substantial area in both cases, for he had a proper sense of fear and was a busy lover. Since he was a clever man and a great lawyer he was able to retire from those areas in wonderfully good order, but at length he was asked to

retreat from that final area where he located his self. And then this sup-
ple, humorous, unassuming and sophisticated person, set like metal,
was overtaken by an absolutely primitive rigor, and could be no more
budged than a cliff."

More was willing to bend and compromise. He loved his job as
the chancellor—the highest legal officer in the realm—and wanted to
keep it if he could. He loved life and did not want to die. He would do
almost anything for King Henry, his dear friend. *But he would not sacrifice his sense of self—not even for the king.* As he tells his wife, who pleads
with him to give in to Henry, "there's a little…little area…where I must
rule myself." And so he quits his job when he cannot go on and refuses
to sign the oath when he cannot in good conscience put his name to it.

It is revealing to compare More with his closest friend, Norfolk.
Norfolk is a decent man. Several times he tries to convince More to
save himself by signing the oath. But like Ivan Ilyich, Norfolk lacks a
fundamental core of self-identity. More recognizes this and confronts
his friend, "Is there no single sinew in the midst of this that serves no
appetite of Norfolk's but is just Norfolk?" Is there no first person, no I,
beneath the social roles and obligations, beneath the masks we wear in
public? Is there nothing that Norfolk himself believes in, that Norfolk
himself cares enough about to stand up for against society?

While More is willing to use his well-honed lawyer's mind to
avoid trouble, and willing to compromise as much as possible, he will
not give up his sense of self because he knows that in the end this is all
he has to give to his God. If he forsakes this, he betrays his soul, for, as
he says, "a man's soul is his self!" For More, the consequence of perjury
is eternal damnation, so he cannot put his name to an oath that he does
not believe. When Norfolk pleads with More to take the oath out of
friendship, More replies, "And when we stand before God, and you are
sent to Paradise for doing according to your conscience, and I am
damned for not doing according to mine, will you come with me, for
fellowship?" No job, no king, no friend can demand this much.

## THE NECESSITY AND INEVITABILITY OF CHOICE

The lesson of Thomas More's life is not that he refused to sign the
king's oath, but that he was willing to draw a line *somewhere.* He was
not willing to surrender his whole self to anyone or anything. With
modern lawyers, so much attention is given to interpreting the rules of
ethics, to determining with mathematical precision whether a certain
act is prohibited or permitted, that a prior and more fundamental
moral issue is often overlooked—more basic than the question whether

or not to do a certain thing is the recognition that some things should be done and others should not.

Let me be clear about what I am saying. I am not suggesting that it is irrelevant or unimportant how a lawyer resolves specific ethical issues such as a conflict of interest or a question of confidentiality. What I am saying is that although we might differ about where to draw the line in such matters, living a moral life depends upon an acknowledgement that lines must be drawn, choices must be made. It is this prior commitment that makes a moral life possible.

James Burtchaell makes this point well: "Thomas More decided at a certain point that he could no longer follow his king. Why at that particular point?...Another man of equal integrity might have said, 'I will go no further,' over another issue, earlier or later than More did. But he *chose*. It was not the intrinsic necessity of events that forced him to draw the line at this point, but it was a necessity for him as an ethical man to pick his breaking point and to stay by his decision....He had to choose."[4]

Burtchaell's analysis brings to mind a lecture I heard in divinity school on Jesus' enigmatic teaching about the Christian's relation to the secular powers: "Render to Caesar what is Caesar's and to God what is God's" (Mk 12:13-17). What precisely is for Caesar and what is reserved for God has bedeviled and divided Christians ever since. But, said the lecturer, that perennial disagreement is less important than the unspoken agreement—an agreement so taken for granted it is rarely even noticed—that *not everything* is for Caesar, that the Christian owes allegiance and loyalty to some power other than the state. Where we draw the line between Caesar and God is open to debate, but ultimately that is not as important as the consensus among Christians that a line must be drawn.

In *A Man for All Seasons*, however, most of the characters cannot understand More's decision because they cannot imagine refusing to do something that society and those in power want done. "When the King wants something done, I do it." They have not reserved any area for themselves and so no lines need be drawn. They are like lawyers so enamored of the adversary system and the game of litigation that they come to see themselves as their client's hired gun whose only job is to do whatever the client wants, no questions asked.

More, in contrast, understands the risk of losing sight of our private self because of our professional obligations. He says, "Well...I believe, when statesmen forsake their private conscience for the sake of their public duties...they lead their country by a short route to chaos."

The risk of such a course is not only social chaos, but the moral collapse of the individual. If a lawyer or anyone else jettisons all moral values at work, then over time those values will dry up. As More says to his accusers, "What you have hunted me for is not my actions, but the thoughts of my heart. It is a long road you have opened. For first men will disclaim their hearts and presently they will have no hearts." First we bracket or ignore our moral values, then they are no longer there when we need them.

I have talked of the necessity of making choices, of drawing lines, of balancing professional duties and personal moral values. More's story also illustrates the paradoxical truth that the moral life is not so much a matter of choice as of a certain vision or character. Christian ethicist Stanley Hauerwas reminds us that in many of our important "choices" there is really no "choice" to be made. Because of who we are, because of who we aspire to be, certain choices are inevitable, and others are unthinkable. Hauerwas applies this insight to More: "Thomas More did not choose to die at the hands of Henry. He did everything he could to avoid having Henry put him to death, not only for his own sake but also because he wished to spare Henry from that task. But he could not take the oath of succession and as a result he had to die. He did not understand that he had thereby made a "decision" needing justification, deontologically or consequentially. He simply did what he had to do."[5]

As More says to a family member who applauds his "noble gesture" of resigning, "It wasn't possible to continue, Will, I was not *able* to continue. I would have if I could! I make no gesture!" More could not have chosen otherwise and been the person he was. His course of action depended far more on who he was than on what he "chose" or "decided."

Once again, as with Ivan Ilyich, we see that the moral life is at least as much a matter of character as of decisions, of "who should I be?" as much as "what should I do?" Indeed, there is a strong case to be made that character precedes choice. I must have a sense of the kind of person I am and hope to be if I am to decide what to do in a particular case. More could not decide whether to resign his office or whether to sign the oath without some inner sense of who he was and where his ultimate loyalty lay.

## FIRST THINGS FIRST

Although More is a man of many conflicting loyalties, there is no doubt that his ultimate loyalty is to God. Not that he has any special insight into God's ways. Like all of us, More must fumble in the dark, following a mysterious God whose ways are not our ways. As he says early in the play, "God's my God. But I find him rather too subtle...I don't know where he is nor what he wants."

Yet despite this rare moment of bitterness, More does know this much about his God: God is the creator who gave human beings a mind to use, and so by using our intellect we serve our God. Part of the reason for More's appeal to lawyers is his legalistic (in the good sense of the word!) approach to the problem of the oath. An oath is composed of words, he says, and he will sign it if he can, if the words permit him. He is no plastic saint; he wants very much to live, and he will use his mind to escape punishment if it is possible to do so. As he says to his family: "God made the angels to show him splendor—as he made animals for innocence and plants for their simplicity. But Man he made for to serve him wittily, in the tangle of his mind!...Our natural business lies in escaping—so let's get home and study this Bill."

The response of my students to this scene is interesting. Many believe that it detracts in some way from More's heroism. In their eyes, More loses some of his luster because of his reluctance to oppose the king. His martyrdom, they feel, is cheapened by his quite human desire to escape death. Surely a true martyr goes to the lions singing hymns to Christ and showering forgiveness on his persecutors!

My feelings are different. More is a model for us precisely because he is a real person, one who—like us—wants to live and succeed. And he is a model for lawyers because he recognizes that his legal skills are a gift from God and realizes that he can serve his God "wittily, in the tangle of his mind."

Like any good lawyer, More recognizes the important role law plays in society as a check against unbridled self-interest and the tyranny of the weak by the strong. At one point, his family inveighs against Richard Rich, More's former friend, who will ultimately prove to be his chief accuser. His family demands that More have Rich arrested, but More insists on following the letter of the law. Roper exclaims, "You'd give the benefit of the doubt to the devil himself!" When More agrees, Roper proclaims that he would cut down every law in England to get at the devil. More responds: "Oh? And when the last law was down, and the Devil turned round on you—where would you hide, Roper, the laws all being flat? This country's planted thick with laws from coast to coast—man's laws, not God's—and if you cut them down—and you're just the man to do it—d'you really think you could stand upright in the winds that would blow then? Yes, I'd give the Devil benefit of law, for my own safety's sake."

Ultimately, of course, the legal system fails More. His enemies trump up charges against him, false accusers come forward, and the law bends to the will of his enemies. A legal system is only as good as the people who make it up.

Yet in the end, when there is no way to escape his fate, More is able to remain faithful to his God even when his other loyalties fail him. He has a place to stand even when the legal system crumbles underfoot. This is because his faith in God is not dependent upon things turning out right. He has the strength to stand firm because he understands that by being faithful to his God he is being faithful to his deepest and best self. In the mystery of faith, God and the human self come together. As More says to Norfolk, "[O]nly God is love right through, Howard, and *that's* my *self*."

For us, too, it is a question of where to place our loyalty. There are many gods who demand our worship. Some are disguised as country or money or honor. Some tempt us under the guise of altruism or service. Sometimes it is our clients, or our courts, or our profession that we turn into gods. This or that deserves our ultimate loyalty, we convince ourselves.

But deep down, where it really matters, we know that none of these lesser gods can save us. Deep down, we know, it is a matter of following the one true God who encompasses and relativizes all other loyalties. As More's life and death teaches us, it is a matter of putting first things first.

This is not something we like to hear. It is easier and more comfortable to deceive ourselves into believing that our duties to God are reserved for Sundays. More knows a hard and bitter truth: If God is truly our sovereign, then God's claim is on us always and everywhere. All other loyalties—whether to clients, family, or profession—are finite and limited, or God is not our God.

Near the end of the play, More's beloved daughter Margaret asks him, "But in reason! Haven't you done as much as God can reasonably want?" More can only respond, "Well…finally…it isn't a matter of reason; finally, it's a matter of love."

So it is, for all of us. When all is said and done, loyalty to the one true God is not a matter of ethics, or intelligence, or codes of conduct. It is not a matter of reason. Finally, it is a matter of love.

# EPILOGUE

## Can a Christian Be a Lawyer?

———————— ◆ ————————

Thomas Shaffer asks the question, "Is it possible to be a Christian and a lawyer?" His answer is that it is only possible "if the question remains unsettled—so that the tentative nature of the answer is itself an admonition to attempt in the practice of law more than the practice itself, the conventional professionalism of it, can bear."[1]

Can a Christian be a lawyer? On one level, of course, the question is nonsensical. When we survey the United States, we see thousands of lawyers, hundreds of thousands, who profess the Christian faith. We know empirically that a Christian can be a lawyer.

On another level, however, the question is more difficult than it first appears. Can a Christian be a lawyer while remaining true to her Christian values? Some answer with a resounding "no," those that fall into the model I have termed *Christ Against the Code*. Others answer the question with a defensive how-dare-you "yes," those within the category I call *Christ in Harmony with the Code*. Both extremes fail to take the question seriously, so they have little to contribute to those of us who want to bring together our life as a Christian and our life as a lawyer. Other lawyers try to have their cake and eat it too, voting "yes" with one hand and "no" with the other—those who fit the model of *Christ in Tension with the Code*.

Throughout this book, I have rejected such unsatisfactory approaches and argued instead for a different vision of the Christian's relationship to the legal system, what I call *Christ Transforming the Code*, or the *Transformist Model*. This model takes Shaffer's question seriously. It recognizes that there is often a gap between our faith and our work, so that the two seem to inhabit separate worlds with little influence upon each other. It admits that the gospel can sometimes stand in tension with the practice and profession of law.

Our challenge, then, is one of balance, of integration. It is a matter of *religion*, for the original meaning of the word is to tie or bind together. Religion is what ties our life together, gives it backbone, substance, meaning. The question is whether we will allow our deepest values and commitments to really influence our daily life. The central mes-

125

sage of this book has been that faith and work belong together, that cross-fertilization is better than rigid separation.

I have spoken often of the dangers of compartmentalizing our lives. I recognize, of course, that a certain compartmentalization is necessary in the modern world. While at work I concentrate on my work, and while playing with my children I try—not always successfully—to keep the focus on my children. But the compartmentalization I decry is of a more sinister sort. It is the type that builds walls between the parts of our lives, walls without doors or windows, so that we become not one person with many roles and responsibilities, but several different persons depending upon the specific role and function we fulfill.

It is this type of compartmentalization that leads to the all-too-common occurrence of devout church-going believers who leave their religious values at the altar and who cannot fathom how or why their Christian values might influence their relationships with clients, colleagues, money, or time.

On the other hand, if I begin to bring my religious values with me into the workplace, a curious thing happens. My work is placed in a wider, deeper frame of meaning. No longer am I a lawyer who happens to be a Christian on Sunday, but a follower of Christ who is trying to live out my Christian calling within my role as a lawyer. It is a small shift, just a rearrangement of a few words, to move from *a lawyer who is a Christian* to *a Christian who is a lawyer*, but in that small shift a whole new way of looking at work emerges, as I open myself to the transforming power of the gospel.

As I dismantle the walls that have divided up my life, I become increasingly attentive to the presence of God and the opportunities for ministry in my daily life and work. I still have many roles to play—I am a spouse, perhaps, and a parent, among other things—but wherever I am and whatever I do, I am one person, not several, struggling to be faithful to God, making mistakes and falling into sin, but redeemed by God's grace, and striving to live out the gospel values of love, forgiveness, and justice.

And so I am not first of all a lawyer, spouse, friend, or parent. First of all I am a disciple of Christ. My ultimate allegiance is not to the things of this world, but to the one true God who transcends all earthly loyalties. Remembering this, I try to approach my work not just as a career but as a calling; I seek to be both companion and prophet to my clients; I recognize an obligation to work for justice for my clients and for society; I see myself not as a hired gun but as a healer of human conflict; I am concerned for the effects of my actions upon third persons and opponents—I do these things not only because they are right in and of themselves, although they are, but because they are indispensable threads in the warp and the woof of the life I am weaving.

Shaffer suggests that the question whether we can be a Christian and a lawyer can only be answered if it remains open-ended, unresolved. If every day we approach the question anew, never certain of the answer, but always taking it seriously, then by that simple act we assure that there will be no neat and artificial compartments in our life. To be a Christian and a lawyer is our constant goal as well as our present reality.

What, then, is the *lawyer's calling*? Perhaps it is simply to acknowledge that our work has spiritual significance, that we are called to serve God and each other in everything we do, not only at work, to be sure, but here as everywhere else. To build a bridge over the chasm that for too long has separated our faith and our work, and to take that first small, shaky step toward bringing the two together.

We will never succeed completely. There will always be an irreducible tension between our faith and our work. There will always be a gap between what we profess and what we do. But that is no reason not to begin. After all, we are not alone. God is with us—that is the meaning of the name Emmanuel—and with God's grace we can begin to see our work as a spiritual journey rich in opportunities for serving God and neighbor. This is our goal. This is our challenge. This is our calling.

# NOTES

## INTRODUCTION

1. Thomas L. Shaffer, *On Being a Christian and a Lawyer: Law for the Innocent* (Provo, Utah: Brigham Young University Press, 1981), p. 166.
2. Mary Ann Glendon, *A Nation Under Lawyers: How the Crisis in the Legal Profession Is Transforming American Society* (New York: Farrar, Straus, and Giroux, 1994), p. 14.
3. These statistics are taken from Glendon, p. 87; Benjamin Sells, *The Soul of the Law* (Rockport, Mass.: Element, 1994), pp. 99-100, 189; and Randall Samborn, "Anti-Lawyer Attitude Up," *The National Law Journal*, August 9, 1993, pp. 1, 20, 22, 24.
4. Anthony T. Kronman, *The Lost Lawyer: Failing Ideals of the Legal Profession* (Cambridge: The Belknap Press of Harvard University Press, 1993), p. 2.
5. Law is not alone in needing to reconnect with its spiritual roots. In a way, this is the great problem facing all work in our time: How can we find the link between our work and our spiritual life? How can we open ourselves to the opportunities for love and service—for ministry—in our jobs? Although this book focuses on the legal profession, it can easily be adapted for other workers—doctors, business executives, farmers, and secretaries. All that is needed is a willingness to confront the gap between our work and our values, and a desire to explore creative ways to bridge that gap.

## CHAPTER 1

1. Sallie McFague, *Models of God: Theology for an Ecological Nuclear Age* (Philadelphia: Fortress Press, 1987). Because language helps shape reality, I have taken pains to avoid identifying all lawyers and clients as male. Instead, I will alternate between masculine and feminine pronouns.
2. Avery Dulles, *Models of the Church* (Garden City, N.Y.: Doubleday, 1974); *Models of Revelation* (Garden City, N.Y.: Doubleday, 1983).
3. H. Richard Niebuhr, *Christ and Culture* (New York: Harper & Row, 1951).

4. Willlam F. May, *The Physician's Covenant: Images of the Healer in Medical Ethics* (Philadelphia: Westminster Press, 1983).

5. My discussion of the models of the Christian lawyer is based in part on my earlier article, "Christ and the Code: The Dilemma of the Christian Lawyer," *The Catholic Lawyer* 34 (1988), pp. 131-141.

6. There are several excellent resources available for analyzing the codes of professional responsibility. For example, Geoffrey C. Hazard, Jr., and W. William Hodes, *The Law of Lawyering: A Handbook on the Model Rules of Professional Conduct*, 2nd ed., 2 vols. (Englewood Cliffs, N.J.: Prentice-Hall Law & Business, 1990, with annual supplements), and Charles W. Wolfram, *Modern Legal Ethics* (St. Paul, Minn.: West Publishing Co., 1986).

7. Gerald J. Postema, "Moral Responsibility in Professional Ethics," *New York University Law Review* 55 (1980), pp. 63-89. A good discussion of the standard vision is found in Deborah L. Rhode and David Luban, *Legal Ethics*, 2nd ed. (Westbury, N.Y.: Foundation Press, 1995), chapter 4.

8. All biblical quotations are from the New Revised Standard Version, unless indicated otherwise.

9. Those who have read Niebuhr are aware that he also identifies a model he calls *Christ Above Culture*. That model is so similar to the *Christ of Culture* type that we need not consider it separately.

10. Niebuhr, p. 41.

11. The answer is *yes, I would*. No matter what our occupation, we can always ask whether there is a tension between our religous values and our work. Of course, the specific issues—we might say the specific temptations—differ from job to job, but the central question remains the same: Am I acting consistently with my Christian values and loyalties?

12. Niebuhr, p. 105.

13. Niebuhr, p. 110.

14. Richard Wasserstrom, "Lawyers as Professionals: Some Moral Issues," *Human Rights* 5 (1975), p. 6.

15. Niebuhr, p. 115.

16. Niebuhr, p. 42.

17. Paul Althaus, *The Ethics of Martin Luther* (Philadelphia: Fortress Press, 1972), pp. 68-69.

18. For an excellent overview of Luther's theology of the two kingdoms, see Althaus, pp. 43-82.

19. Erwin Chemerinsky, "Protecting Lawyers From Their Profession: Redefining the Lawyer's Role," *The Journal of the Legal Profession* 5 (1980), pp. 31-43.

20. James Luther Adams, *The Prophethood of All Believers* (Boston: Beacon Press, 1986), p. 152.

21. Niebuhr, p. 209.

22. James A. Pike, *Beyond the Law: The Religious and Ethical Meaning of the Lawyer's Vocation* (Garden City, N.Y.: Doubleday & Co., 1963), p. 24.

## CHAPTER 2

1. Dennis M. Campbell, *Doctors, Lawyers, Ministers: Christian Ethics in Professional Practice* (Nashville: Abingdon, 1982), p. 17.

2. For a brief overview of the history of the professions, see Campbell, pp. 17-21, and Stephen F. Barker, "What Is a Profession?" *Professional Ethics* 1 (1992), pp. 73-99. The quote from Barker is on p. 86.

3. Richard Wasserstrom, "Lawyers as Professionals: Some Moral Issues," *Human Rights* 5 (1975), p. 2. The language and arrangement are my own, based upon Wasserstrom's categories.

4. Roscoe Pound, *The Lawyer from Antiquity to Modern Times* (St. Paul, Minn.: West Publishing Co., 1953), p. 5.

5. Charles Kammer,"Vocation and the Professions," in *The Annual of the Society of Christian Ethics*, ed. Thomas W. Ogletree, pp. 153-183, 1981. My discussion of the idea of vocation owes much to Kammer and to Lee Hardy, *The Fabric of This World: Inquiries into Calling, Career Choice, and the Design of Human Work* (Grand Rapids, Mich.: Eerdmans Publishing Co., 1990).

6. Hardy, p. 24.

7. Kammer, p. 170.

8. Quoted in Hardy, p. 56.

9. Paul Althaus, *The Ethics of Martin Luther* (Philadelphia: Fortress Press, 1972), p. 10.

10. Hardy, p. 67.

11. Quoted in Hardy, p. 72.

12. *On Human Work: A Resource Book for the Study of Pope John Paul II's Third Encyclical* (Washington, D.C.: United States Catholic Conference, 1982), p. 52.

13. James Gustafson, "Professions as Callings," *Social Service Review* (December 1982), p. 508. The following quotation is from Gustafson, p. 511.

14. John Calvin, *Institutes of the Christian Religion*, 2 vols., ed. John T. McNeill (Philadelphia: Westminster Press, 1960). Calvin's discussion of calling appears in vol. 2 at pp. 1062-1068. All quotations are from that source.

15. Gustafson, p. 511.

16. Kammer, p. 174.

17. Even if the client is an organization such as a corporation, the lawyer can only deal with it through real-life human beings.

18. Robert N. Bellah, Richard Madsen, William M. Sullivan, Ann Swidler, Steven M. Tipton, *Habits of the Heart: Individualism and Commitment in American Life* (New York: Harper & Row, 1985), p. 71.

## CHAPTER 3

1. Or, as Professor Stephen Gillers puts it, "In the beginning is the client." Gillers, *Regulation of Lawyers: Problems of Law and Ethics*, 4th ed. (Boston: Little, Brown & Co., 1995), p. 15.

2. My discussion of the covenantal relationship between lawyers and clients, and the differences between covenant and contract, owes much to William F. May, *The Physician's Covenant: Images of the Healer in Medical Ethics* (Philadelphia: Westminster Press, 1983).

3. Douglas E. Rosenthal, *Lawyer and Client: Who's in Charge?* (New York: Russell Sage Foundation, 1974), p. 7.

4. In my discussion of the factors contributing to lawyer dominance, I have relied especially upon Richard Wasserstrom, "Lawyers as Professionals: Some Moral Issues," *Human Rights* 5 (1975), pp. 1-24, and upon Christopher F. Mooney, S.J., "Law: A Vocation to Love and Justice," in *The Professions in Ethical Context: Vocations to Justice and Love*, ed. Francis A. Figo, pp. 59-95 (Villanova, Pa.: Villanova University Press, 1986).

5. Wasserstrom, p. 18.

6. Joseph L. Allen, *Love and Conflict: A Covenantal Model of Christian Ethics* (Nashville: Abingdon Press, 1984), p. 18. Allen's book is probably the best examination of the theme of covenant for the general reader. My own discussion owes much to him.

7. Allen, p. 66.

8. Allen, pp. 74-81.

9. Allen, p. 33.

10. Allen, p. 37.

11. Thomas L. Shaffer, *On Being a Christian and a Lawyer: Law for the Innocent* (Provo, Utah: Brigham Young Press, 1981), p. 37.

12. May, p. 115.

13. It is a sad but telling fact about the professional impulse toward dominance that almost everyone can recount incidents of physicians treating them less as adults than as children or objects. People who have dealt with lawyers often have similar stories to tell.

14. Some legal scholars have analogized the lawyer-client relationship to the relationship between friends. The most well-known argument

along these lines is Charles Fried, "The Lawyer as Friend: The Moral Foundations of the Lawyer-Client Relation," *Yale Law Journal* 85 (1976), pp. 1060-1089. I will have more to say about the analogy to friendship in the next chapter when I discuss the prophetic dimension of the lawyer-client covenant.

15. Allen, p. 37.

16. Shaffer, pp. 28-29.

17. Karl Barth, *The Humanity of God* (Richmond: John Knox Press, 1960), pp. 86-87.

18. Benjamin Sells, *The Soul of the Law* (Rockport, Mass.: Element, 1994), p. 62.

19. May, p. 120.

20. May, pp. 123-124.

21. Allen, p. 38.

22. There is some evidence that client outcomes are better when lawyers and clients work together than when the lawyer simply assumes command of the representation. See Rosenthal.

### CHAPTER 4

1. Quoted in Mary Ann Glendon, *A Nation Under Lawyers: How the Crisis in the Legal Profession Is Transforming American Society* (New York: Farrar, Straus, and Giroux, 1994), p. 37.

2. Walter Brueggemann, *The Prophetic Imagination* (Philadelphia: Fortress Press, 1978), p. 23.

3. Thomas Shaffer reports using a similar hypothetical in his law school classes. Shaffer's example is of an elderly woman who wants to disinherit her entire family and leave her estate to the Christian Anti-Communist Crusade. After working through the legal issues of how to redraft a will to suit a client's changed objectives, Shaffer asks his students, "Now that you know you could do this for a client, I wonder whether you would do it." *On Being a Christian and a Lawyer: Law for the Innocent* (Provo, Utah: Brigham Young Press, 1981), pp. 3-4.

4. Thomas L. Shaffer, "Legal Ethics and the Good Client," *Catholic University Law Review* 36 (1987), pp. 329-330.

5. See Joseph Allegretti, "Shooting Elephants, Serving Clients: An Essay on George Orwell and the Lawyer-Client Relationship," *Creighton Law Review* 27 (1993), pp. 1-24.

6. See the discussion of prophets in Shaffer, *On Being a Christian and a Lawyer*, chapter 10.

7. Some lawyers, of course, serve as in-house counsel for a company. A lawyer in that situation might find it more difficult to speak propheti-

cally than a lawyer who is an outside practitioner, because the in-house counsel is an employee who draws a paycheck from the client and whose success in the company depends upon how well she gets along with management. On the other hand, outside lawyers may fear losing a client if they say "no," so they too are under pressure to tailor their advice to meet their client's desires. In-house counsel does possess an advantage over the outside practitioner: She has more of an opportunity to develop a close personal relationship with her client, which is the necessary prerequisite for prophetic ministry. And the very fact that in-house counsel is employed to give *legal advice* provides some independence from the client.

8. Abraham J. Heschel, *The Prophets: An Introduction*, Harper Torchbooks ed., vol. 1 (New York: Harper and Row, 1969), pp. 204-205.

9. Heschel, p. 204.

## CHAPTER 5

1. Sam Benson, "Why I Quit Practicing Law," *Newsweek*, November 4, 1991, p. 10.

2. Sol M. Linowitz with Martin Mayer, *The Betrayed Profession: Lawyering at the End of the Twentieth Century* (New York: Charles Scribner's Sons, 1994), p. 192. A 1992 survey of women lawyers found that only fifty-four percent of the respondents would have become lawyers if they had known ten years earlier what they now knew about the practice of law. Linowitz, p. 242.

3. Lord Brougham is quoted in David Mellinkoff, *The Conscience of a Lawyer* (St. Paul, Minn.: West Publishing Co., 1973), pp. 188-189. Much of my discussion of the hired gun is based upon Joseph Allegretti, "Have Briefcase Will Travel: The Lawyer as Hired Gun," *Creighton University Law Review* 24 (1991), pp. 747-780.

4. Charles W. Wolfram, *Modern Legal Ethics* (St. Paul, Minn.: West Publishing Co., 1986), p. 580. The following quotation is from the same source.

5. Quoted in Allegretti, pp. 776-777.

6. Rudolph J. Gerber, *Lawyers, Courts, and Professionalism: The Agenda for Reform* (Westport, Conn.: Greenwood Press, 1989), p. 86.

7. Wayne D. Brazil, "The Attorney as Victim: Toward More Candor About the Psychological Price Tag of Litigation Practice," Journal of the Legal Profession 3 (1978-1979), pp. 107-117.

8. Brazil, p. 116.

9. Milner S. Ball, *Lying Down Together: Law, Metaphor, and Theology* (Madison, Wis.: University of Wisconsin Press, 1985), p. 22.

10. For a discussion of a number of "ethical identities" of lawyers, see Richard O. Brooks, "Ethical Legal Identity and Professional Responsibility," *Georgetown Journal of Legal Ethics* 4 (1990), pp. 317-369.

11. Quoted in Allegretti, p. 778.

12. Richard Wasserstrom, "Lawyers as Professionals: Some Moral Issues," *Human Rights* 5 (1975), p. 6.

13. Robert Bolt, *A Man for All Seasons* (New York: Vintage Books, 1962), pp. 76-77. I examine More's life in more detail in Chapter 8.

14. I focus on the criminal defense context, but many of the same issues arise when a lawyer represents a defendant in a civil action. A lawyer could "know," for example, that her client ran a stoplight and caused the accident that gave rise to the lawsuit. Some of the same justifications that apply in the criminal context are relevant here, although some scholars feel that the arguments in favor of representing the guilty are more weighty in criminal cases than civil.

15. Geoffrey C. Hazard, Jr., and W. William Hodes, *The Law of Lawyering: A Handbook on the Model Rules of Professional Conduct*, 2nd ed., 2 vols. (Englewood Cliffs, N.J.: Prentice-Hall Law & Business, 1990, with annual supplements), p. lxxix.

16. Bolt, p. 38.

17. Jack L. Sammons, Jr., *Lawyer Professionalism* (Durham, N.C.: Carolina Academic Press, 1988), pp. 49-54. The following quotation is at p. 52.

18. Thomas L. Shaffer, *On Being a Christian and a Lawyer: Law for the Innocent* (Provo: Brigham Young Press, 1981), p. 50.

19. My analysis owes much to Stanley Hauerwas, *The Peaceable Kingdom: A Primer in Christian Ethics* (Notre Dame, Ind.: University of Notre Dame Press, 1983), especially chapter 5.

20. Shaffer, p. 78.

21. Adapted from Shaffer, p. 56.

22. William Stringfellow, "A Lawyer's Work," *Christian Legal Society Quarterly* 3, no. 3 (1982), p. 19. At the same time, however, Stringfellow was pessimistic about the possibility of being both a Christian activist and a lawyer, and admitted that he was "haunted with the ironic impression that I may have to renounce being a lawyer the better to be an advocate."

23. Brian J. Peterson, "The Criminal Justice System Wants: YOU," *Christian Legal Society Quarterly* 2, no. 3 (1981), pp. 21-22.

24. Peterson, p. 21, quoting Lk 4:18.

25. Peterson, p. 22.

26. Lon L. Fuller and John D. Randall, "Professional Responsibility:

Report of the Joint Conference of the ABA and the AALS," *American Bar Association Journal* 44 (December 1958), pp. 1161-1162.

27. Mark Curriden, "The Lies Have It," *American Bar Association Journal* 81 (May 1995), pp. 68-72. This article includes an overview of the relevant codes of professional responsibility that apply to perjury.

28. Curriden, p. 69, quoting David C. Weiner, the chairperson of the American Bar Association Litigation Section.

## CHAPTER 6

1. Filings of lawsuits in the federal courts tripled between 1960 and 1990. Mary Ann Glendon, *A Nation Under Lawyers: How the Crisis in the Legal Profession Is Transforming American Society* (New York: Farrar, Straus, Giroux, 1994), p. 53. Not all scholars agree that there is too much litigation in America. For an overview of the debate, see Deborah L. Rhode and David Luban, *Legal Ethics*, 2nd ed. (Westbury, N.Y.: Foundation Press, 1995), pp. 711-726.

2. Rudolph J. Gerber, *Lawyers, Courts, and Professionalism: The Agenda for Reform* (Westport, Conn.: Greenwood Press, 1989), p. 3.

3. Warren Burger, "Isn't There A Better Way? Annual Report of the Judiciary (January 24, 1982)," quoted in Leonard L. Riskin and James E. Westbrook, *Dispute Resolution and Lawyers*, abridged version (St. Paul, Minn.: West Publishing Co., 1988), p. 9.

4. Benjamin Sells, *The Soul of the Law* (Rockport, Mass.: Element: 1994), pp. 86-89.

5. Abraham J. Heschel, *The Prophets: An Introduction*, Harper Torchbooks ed., vol. 1 (New York: Harper and Row, 1969), pp. 204-205.

6. Quoted in Rev. Vincent P. Mainelli, ed., *Official Catholic Teachings: Social Justice* (Wilmington, N.C.: McGrath Publishing Company, 1978), p. 312.

7. Verses 9-11 are often read as a conclusion to Paul's exhortation on litigation.

8. See Ken Sande, *The Peacemaker: A Biblical Guide to Resolving Personal Conflict* (Grand Rapids, Mich.: Baker Book House, 1991), pp. 221-226.

9. Robert D. Taylor, "Toward a Biblical Theology of Litigation: A Law Professor Looks at I Cor. 6:1-11," *Ex Auditu* 2 (1986), pp. 105-116. I am indebted to Taylor for the labels "pro-mediation" and "anti-litigation" to express the core of Paul's teaching on litigation.

10. Taylor, p. 106.

11. Taylor, p. 108.

12. My discussion of Calvin is based upon my earlier article, "'In All This Love Will Be the Best Guide': John Calvin on the Christian's

Resort to the Secular Legal System," *The Journal of Law and Religion* 9 (1991), pp. 1-16.

A word on sources. Calvin discusses 1 Corinthians 6 in his great work Institutes of the Christian Religion, 2 vols., ed. John T. McNeill (Philadelphia: Westminster Press, 2 vols., 1960), in volume 2 at pp. 1505-1509, and in his commentary on 1 Corinthians, Calvin's Commentaries—The First Epistle of Paul the Apostle to the Corinthians, ed. David W. and Thomas F. Torrance (Edinburgh: Oliver & Boyd, 1960), at pp. 117-122. All references to and quotations from Calvin are from these two sources.

13. Taylor, p. 111.
14. Taylor, p. 109.
15. Robert Cover, "Violence and the Word," *Yale Law Journal* 95 (1986), pp. 1601-1629. The following two quotations are from Cover, p. 1609 and p. 1601.
16. Taylor, pp. 109-110.
17. National Conference of Catholic Bishops, *The Challenge of Peace: God's Promise and Our Response* (Washington, D.C.: United States Catholic Conference, 1983). The conditions for a just war that I discuss are found at pp. 36-48.
18. Quoted in Richard A. Zitrin and Carol M. Langford, *Legal Ethics in the Practice of Law* (Charlottesville, Va.: Michie Co., 1995), p. 238.
19. I have been examining cases in which the question is whether or not to bring a lawsuit. But the same approach should guide lawyers and clients when they are defendants in a lawsuit. Again, lawyers should urge their clients to examine their reasons for resisting the claim, to consider the costs and likely consequences of defending the lawsuit, and to explore possible alternatives to litigation.
20. See, for example, the work of the Institute for Christian Conciliation, which seeks to resolve conflicts according to biblical principles. The Institute can be reached at 1537 Avenue D, Suite 352, Billings, Montana, 59102.
21. Matthew 18:15-18: "If another member of the church sins against you, go and point out the fault when the two of you are alone. If the member listens to you, you have regained that one. But if you are not listened to, take one or two others along with you, so that every word may be confirmed by the evidence of two or three witnesses. If the member refuses to listen to them, tell it to the church; and if the offender refuses to listen even to the church, let such a one be to you as a Gentile and a tax collector." See Lynn R. Buzzard and Laurence Eck, *Tell It to the Church: Reconciling Out of Court* (Elgin, Ill.: David C. Cook Publishing Co., 1982).

22. *Christian Conciliation Handbook* (Billings, Mont.: Institute for Christian Conciliation, 1994), Rules of Procedure for Christian Conciliation, Rule 1, p. 17.

23. Quoted in *Christian Conciliation Handbook*, p. 10.

## CHAPTER 7

1. John Calvin, *Calvin's Commentaries—The First Epistle of Paul the Apostle to the Corinthians*, ed. David W. and Thomas F. Torrance (Edinburgh: Oliver & Boyd, 1960), p. 122.

2. Much of the following discussion in this chapter is based upon my article, Joseph Allegretti, "Rights, Roles, Relationships: The Wisdom of Solomon and the Ethics of Lawyers," *Creighton Law Review* 25 (1992), pp. 1119-1139.

3. Rand Jack and Dana Crowley Jack, *Moral Vision and Professional Decisions: The Changing Values of Women and Men Lawyers* (Cambridge: Cambridge University Press, 1989).

4. Carol Gilligan, *In a Different Voice: Psychological Theory and Women's Development* (Cambridge, Ma.: Harvard University Press, 1982).

5. The discussion of the divorce hypothetical is in Jack and Jack at pp. 78-85.

6. Jack and Jack, pp. 8-9.

7. Jack and Jack, p. 82.

8. Jack and Jack, p. 126.

9. In retelling the speeches of Solomon and the two women, I have paraphrased the biblical language.

10. Phyllis Trible, *God and the Rhetoric of Sexuality* (Philadelphia: Fortress Press, 1978), p. 32.

11. Trible, p. 32.

12. Richard D. Nelson, *First and Second Kings* (Atlanta: John Knox Press, 1987), pp. 38-39.

13. Gilligan, pp. 104-105.

14. John T. Noonan, Jr., *Persons and Masks of the Law: Cardozo, Holmes, Jefferson, and Wythe as Makers of the Masks* (New York: Farrar, Straus, and Giroux, 1976), p. 18.

15. Joseph L. Allen, *Love and Conflict: A Covenantal Model of Christian Ethics* (Nashville: Abingdon Press, 1984), p. 39.

16. Law professor Stephen Ellmann suggests that a care-oriented lawyer should consider several factors when deciding whether to accept a would-be client: the extent of the client's need, the lawyer's ability or inability to care for the client, and the caring or uncaring nature of the acts the lawyer is being asked to perform. Stephen

Ellmann, "The Ethic of Care as an Ethic for Lawyers," *Georgetown Law Review* 81 (1993), pp. 2665-2726.

17. National Conference of Catholic Bishops, *Economic Justice for All: Pastoral Letter on Catholic Social Teaching and the U.S. Economy* (Washington: United States Catholic Conference, 1986), p. 22.

18. The translation is from Stephen Charles Mott, *Biblical Ethics and Social Change* (New York: Oxford University Press, 1982), p. 63.

19. Mott, pp. 63-64.

20. Noonan, p. 18.

21. Reinhold Niebuhr, *An Interpretation of Christian Ethics* (San Francisco: Harper & Row, 1935), especially chapters 2-4.

### CHAPTER 8

1. Leo Tolstoy, "The Death of Ivan Ilyich," in *The Cossacks/Happy Ever After/The Death of Ivan Ilyich*, transl. Rosemary Edmonds (New York: Penguin Books, 1960), pp. 99-161. All quotations from "The Death of Ivan Ilyich" are from this source.

2. Stanley Hauerwas, *The Peaceable Kingdom: A Primer in Christian Ethics* (Notre Dame, Ind.: University of Notre Dame Press 1983), p. 117.

3. Robert Bolt, *A Man for All Seasons* (New York: Vintage Books, 1960). All quotations from *A Man for All Seasons* are from this source. For a modern biography that deepens our understanding of More, but does not fundamentally contradict his portrait in the play, see Richard Marius, *Thomas More* (New York: Knopf, 1985).

4. James Tunstead Burtchaell, C.S.C., *Philemon's Problem: The Daily Dilemma of the Christian* (Chicago: ACTA Foundation, 1973), p. 90.

5. Hauerwas, p. 129.

### EPILOGUE

1. Thomas L. Shaffer, *On Being a Christian and a Lawyer: Law for the Innocent* (Provo, Utah: Brigham Young University Press, 1981), p. 32.

# BIBLIOGRAPHY

———— ◆ ————

The following books have proven especially helpful to me in my thinking about faith and the practice of law.

Allen, Joseph L. *Love and Conflict: A Covenantal Model of Christian Ethics.* Nashville: Abingdon Press, 1984.

Althaus, Paul. *The Ethics of Martin Luther.* Philadelphia: Fortress Press, 1972.

Ball, Milner S. *The Promise of American Law: A Theological, Humanistic View of Legal Process.* Athens, Ga.: University of Georgia Press, 1981.

———. *The Word and the Law.* Chicago: University of Chicago Press, 1993.

Bellah, Robert N., and Richard Madsen, William M. Sullivan, Ann Swidler, Steven M. Tipton. *Habits of the Heart: Individualism and Commitment in American Life.* New York: Harper & Row, 1985.

Berman, Harold J. *Faith and Order: The Reconciliation of Law and Religion.* Atlanta: Scholars Press, 1993.

Birch, Bruce C., and Larry L. Rasmussen. *Bible & Ethics in the Christian Life.* Revised and Expanded Edition. Minneapolis, Minn.: Augsburg Press, 1989.

Brueggemann, Walter. *The Prophetic Imagination.* Philadelphia: Fortress Press, 1978.

Burtchaell, James Tunstead, C.S.C. *Philemon's Problem: The Daily Dilemma of the Christian.* Chicago: ACTA Foundation, 1973.

Calvin, John. *Calvin's Commentaries—The First Epistle of Paul the Apostle to the Corinthians.* Edited by David W. and Thomas F. Torrance. Edinburgh: Oliver & Boyd, 1960.

———. *Institutes of the Christian Religion.* 2 vols. Edited by John T. McNeill. Philadelphia: Westminster Press, 1960.

Campbell, Dennis M. *Doctors, Lawyers, Ministers: Christian Ethics in Professional Practice.* Nashville: Abingdon, 1982.

139

Droel, William L. *The Spirituality of Work: Lawyers*. Chicago: National Center for the Laity, 1989.

Gerber, Rudolph J. *Lawyers, Courts, and Professionalism: The Agenda for Reform*. Westport, Conn.: Greenwood Press, 1989.

Gilligan, Carol. *In a Different Voice: Psychological Theory and Women's Development*. Cambridge: Harvard University Press, 1982.

Glendon, Mary Ann. *A Nation Under Lawyers: How the Crisis in the Legal Profession Is Transforming American Society*. New York: Farrar, Straus and Giroux, 1994.

Hardy, Lee. *The Fabric of This World: Inquiries into Calling, Career Choice, and the Design of Human Work*. Grand Rapids, Mich.: Eerdmans Publishing Co., 1990.

Hauerwas, Stanley. *The Peaceable Kingdom: A Primer in Christian Ethics*. Notre Dame, Ind.: University of Notre Dame Press, 1983.

Heschel, Abraham J. *The Prophets: An Introduction*. Harper Torchbooks ed. 2 vols. New York: Harper & Row, 1969.

Jack, Rand, and Dana Crowley Jack. *Moral Vision and Professional Decisions: The Changing Values of Women and Men Lawyers*. Cambridge: Cambridge University Press, 1989.

Kelly, Michael J. *Lives of Lawyers: Journeys in the Organizations of Practice*. Ann Arbor, Mich.: University of Michigan Press, 1994.

Kronman, Anthony T. *The Lost Lawyer: Failing Ideals of the Legal Profession*. Cambridge: The Belknap Press of Harvard University Press, 1993.

Linowitz, Sol M. with Martin Mayer. *The Betrayed Profession: Lawyering at the End of the Twentieth Century*. New York: Charles Scribner's Sons, 1994.

Luban, David. *The Good Lawyer: Lawyers' Roles and Lawyers' Ethics*. Totowa, N.J.: Rowman & Allanheld, 1983.

————, ed. *Lawyers and Justice: An Ethical Study*. Princeton, N.J.: Princeton University Press, 1988.

May, William F. *The Physician's Covenant: Images of the Healer in Medical Ethics*. Philadelphia: Westminster Press, 1983.

Mount, Eric, Jr. *Professional Ethics in Context: Institutions, Images, and Empathy*. Louisville, Ky.: Westminster/John Knox Press, 1990.

National Conference of Catholic Bishops. *The Challenge of Peace: God's Promise and Our Response*. Washington, D.C.: United States Catholic Conference, 1983.

———. *Economic Justice for All: Pastoral Letter on Catholic Social Teaching and the U.S. Economy*. Washington, D.C.: United States Catholic Conference, 1986.

Neuhaus, Richard John, ed. *Law and the Ordering of Our Life Together*. Grand Rapids, Mich.: Eerdmans Publishing Co., 1989.

Niebuhr, H. Richard. *Christ and Culture*. New York: Harper & Row, 1951.

Noonan, John T., Jr. *Persons and Masks of the Law: Cardozo, Holmes, Jefferson, and Wythe as Makers of the Masks*. New York: Farrar, Straus, and Giroux, 1976.

*On Human Work: A Resource Book for the Study of Pope John Paul II's Third Encyclical*. Washington, D.C.: United States Catholic Conference, 1982.

Pierce, Gregory F. Augustine, ed. *Of Human Hands: A Reader in the Spirituality of Work*. Minneapolis, Minn.: Augsburg Press, 1991; Chicago: ACTA Publications, 1991.

Pike, James A. *Beyond the Law: The Religious and Ethical Meaning of the Lawyer's Vocation*. Garden City, N.Y.: Doubleday & Co., 1963.

Reeck, Darrell. *Ethics for the Professions: A Christian Perspective*. Minneapolis, Minn.: Augsburg Publishing House, 1982.

Rhode, Deborah L., and David Luban. *Legal Ethics*. 2nd ed. Westbury, N.Y.: Foundation Press, 1995.

Sammons, Jack L., Jr. *Lawyer Professionalism*. Durham, N.C.: Carolina Academic Press, 1988.

Sells, Benjamin. *The Soul of the Law*. Rockport, Mass.: Element, 1994.

Shaffer, Thomas L. *Faith and the Professions*. Provo, Utah: Brigham Young University, 1987.

———. *On Being a Christian and a Lawyer: Law for the Innocent*. Provo, Utah: Brigham Young University Press, 1981.

Shaffer, Thomas L. with Mary M. Shaffer. *American Lawyers and Their Communities: Ethics in the Legal Profession*. Notre Dame, Ind.: University of Notre Dame Press, 1991.